LEARNING & LIVING WITH

autism

A Story of Hope

ELIZABETH C. JEKANOWSKI, PH.D.

dp

Divina Press
an imprint of Lectio Publishing, LLC
Hobe Sound, Fla.

Images and reproductions used with permission.

Cover and Book Design: Linda Wolf

ISBN (Print) 978-1-943901-95-1
Library of Congress Control Number: 2022904059
ISBN (e-Book) 978-1-943901-94-4

Published through Divina Press
an imprint of Lectio Publishing, LLC
Hobe Sound, Florida 33455
www.divinapress.com

DEDICATION

Dedicated with thanksgiving
to a loving God
who moves mountains,
parts the sea,
and blesses us with hope.

CONTENTS

ACKNOWLEDGEMENTS

I am profoundly grateful to all who helped me write this hopeful book about our son with autism. Philip, my loving husband and soulmate, I could not have done this without you! Thank you for your endless support, encouragement, and sharing. Thank you for always believing in me, and in our God who would help us get this book published.

Tom, and Patrick, thank you for the amazing sons you are, the strong men you have become and all the ways you helped. Tom, thank you for permission to share about your life with autism and for your support of this book. Your honest, straightforward, "insider" reflections at the end of each chapter are, as Dr. Scott pens, innovative. Patrick, thank you for your unconditional love for and support of your brother. Thank you for your endless enthusiasm for the project. Your support and encouragement mean more than you will ever know! To my dear niece, Emilie, thank you for creating the first book cover draft with such beauty and love!

To my "everything" editor/publishers, Eric and Linda Wolf of Divina Press, for your anointed expertise, guidance and dedication which have made this book a reality, thank you for everything you did to transform my raw manuscript into its present, polished, published form. Having smoothie luncheons and coffee talks with you, Linda, was very special to me because, in addition to talking about the book, we also spoke of life and faith, as friends. Thank you, forever and ever, to Michael Heron, for you are the angel who connected us to Eric and Linda. Your openness to go to a meeting and introduce yourself to a friend you had not yet met, is a beautiful example of how our God lovingly orchestrates His plans. Thank you.

Thank you to all my colleagues and friends who wrote such beautiful book reviews. Dr. Jack Scott, we are deeply grateful for your writing in praise of our ABA clinical notes and Tom's innovative chapter reflections. It is incredible that you were a contributing author in the book that guided Tom's home program, over twenty years ago. Such a blessing to know you today! Donald Battiston, thank you for all your love and support through the years! Thank you for your enthusiastic book recommendations to religious and deacons to help better understand and serve individuals with autism in our communities. Barb Dixon, thank you, dear friend, for all your love and support! Thank you for your inspiring book recommendation to educators and family members caring for children with autism, in need of hope. Kathy Carr, thank you for your loving work teaching a very young Tom. Thank you for your beautiful words praising God for Tom's success and for untold blessings for all who read this book, you will always have a special place in our hearts. Dr. Ginger Featherstone, thank you for your strong and caring leadership. It was in your high school that Tom developed a confidence and ease with his peers which continues today. It was in your high school that Tom's scholarly identity emerged. Your presence in our lives and book recommendation will forever touch our hearts. Rob Romano, extraordinary teacher, coach, and Driver's Ed instructor, thank you for recommending this book as a gift, as an opportunity to learn from, as you did, "Thomas the Promise."

Thank you to my parents in heaven, Dr. Ted and Joan Collier, for all their love and support always! Thank you to all our very special family, friends and professionals who are included in this book. Each of you played an essential role in supporting Tom's learning and happy life (in the order they appear): Gary Trainor, Nina Lucario, Catherine Stover, Mary Flanagan, Kim Nelson, Lisa Williamson, Marilyn Murray, Andrea Williams, Kathy Carr, Tracy Osbahr, Kim Nelson, Meredith Larrabee, Karen McCullen, Mr. Jym, Anne Dalzell, Linda Sauter, Kit Fruscione, Joanne Murphy, Deb Lawrence, Karen Olswoski, Chuck and Mary Murray, Brittany Jones, Kim Smith, Pat and Sue Bartolone, Pam Aursland, Dr. Ginger Featherstone, Tom Dougherty, James Paul, Meghan Trainor, Rivka Felsher and Maryellen Quinlunney. To all the very special people everywhere, who have been a part of Tom's story, over the years, thank you.

Thank you to the wonderful organizations included in this book (in the order they appear): Nantucket Public Schools/Nantucket Elementary School (Nantucket, MA), Early Intervention of The Cape and Islands (Hyannis, MA), Children's Hospital (Boston, MA), The Department of Developmental Disabilities (formerly Department of Mental Retardation) (Southborough, MA), The New England Center for Children (Southborough, MA), Boston Higashi School—Autism (Randolph, MA), The May Institute (Chatham, MA), The Department of Public Health (North Hampton, MA), St. Mary's, Our Lady of the Isle Catholic Church (Nantucket, MA), Murray Camp (Nantucket, MA), Martin County School District/Jensen Beach Elementary/Stuart Middle/Jensen Beach High (Jensen Beach/Stuart, FL), St. Martin dePorres Catholic Church (Jensen Beach, FL), Florida State University (Tallahassee, FL), Florida Atlantic University (Boca Raton, FL), The Center for Autism and Related Disabilities (CARD), FAU (Boca Raton, FL), Ernie Els for Autism (Jupiter, FL), Vocational Rehabilitation (Stuart, FL; Dubuque, IA), The Town of Jupiter Building Department (Jupiter, FL), Jupiter Medical Center (Jupiter, FL), Phi Beta Kappa Society (Washington, D.C.) and American Customer Care (Dubuque, IA).

To all listed above, and to those forever listed in our hearts—my deepest gratitude! Your love, support and care have, quite simply, made this story of hope, this book possible. Thank you!

INTRODUCTION

This is a remarkable and true story about my son Tom who at twenty-seven months was diagnosed with severe autism. It is a story that has been writing itself for over twenty years! With Tom's permission and blessing, I share his journey chronologically along with actual home program session notes, evaluation data, classwork, artwork, photos, and awards. Each chapter concludes with "Tom's Thoughts" about the material, his memories and thoughts of that time.

I include a brief reflective guide at the end of every chapter. These guides highlight topics in each chapter and are intended for parents, educators, therapists, community members, and even policy makers — anyone who knows, loves and/or works on behalf of children and young adults with autism.

Parent groups, special educators, and teaching groups may use the "big ideas" and related questions to frame a dialogue and examination of their planning and education of children with autism. Tom has benefited greatly over the years from my leading conversations around questions such as these.

Autism is a serious, neurological disorder affecting 1 in 54 children in the United States today (www.cdc.gov/ncbddd/autism/data.html). Autism Spectrum Disorder usually manifests by 2-3 years of age and is characterized by delays in speech, and difficulties with social skills, repetitive behaviors

1

and nonverbal communication.

The prognosis for those severely affected is poor. According to sources1, close to a million teens will enter adulthood each year without ever having held a paying job.

"Over the next decade, an estimated 707,000 to 1,116,000 teens each year will enter adulthood and age out of school-based autism services. Nearly half of 25-year-olds with autism have never held a paying job." (autismspeaks.org/autism-statistics)

This is a story of hope for the families with children newly diagnosed with autism, and encouragement for those who are a few years, or maybe many years, into intensive educational and therapeutic programming. It is a story of affirmation for (and an expression of gratitude to) all families and professionals working with children and young adults with autism. This is Tom's story. He is letting me share his journey now because he believes that many people will benefit. It may be one thing or it may be an affirmation of many things—but whatever it is, sharing his story with you will be worth it!

TOM'S THOUGHTS

My life has been an incredible journey, both literally and metaphorically. It has been an odyssey—I was told, to go from a child whose best hope might have been an institutionalized life to where I am today. I have also lived and been to many parts of the United States in my life. For instance, I have lived on Nantucket Island, Jensen Beach, Florida, on campus at FSU and FAU and am currently living in Dubuque, Iowa. Over many family and school trips, I've been to the Grand Canyon, Bryce Canyon, Disney World (at least a few times), New York City (twice), San Diego (Pacific Oceanside for first time) Atlanta, and many others. Throughout each chapter of this book, I will record my reflections/memories of these times in my life mentioned. My memories of some of these events may be fuzzy, so I will try to be as accurate as possible.

CHAPTER ONE

Waking Up

Family & Friends' Concerns

Tom was a beautiful baby. Soft red hair, big green eyes, and very content. He nursed easily, slept through the night and was content just to be in my arms, on my lap or nearby while I prepared a meal or did the laundry. I was in love with being a mom, totally unaware that Tom was behind—after all, he walked at 10 months. At Tom's 24-month check-up, the pediatrician assured us that his lack of babbling was most likely due to having a very active and talkative older brother. We all thought that Tom's silence was just part of his placid personality.

Tom 2 years old

Soon after Tom's second birthday, our nephew Gary, who had experience with special education, told us he was concerned about Tom. He was worried about Tom's lack of eye contact and speech delay. Gary had talked about Tom with his good friend, the Director of Special Education in our local school district. She offered to contact us with advice about the next steps. My husband Phil and I were stunned, although in truth we were beginning to wonder too. Just the day before, my husband had been doing dishes in the kitchen and Tom started banging his head against his leg. He asked me what was going on. I didn't know. Pondering Gary's words, knowing we would be getting a phone call from the Director by the end of the week, I knew that I had to get out of the house. I put the boys in the double stroller and went for a long walk.

Our house was about a mile from the center of town. When I got to main street with the stroller, I saw Catherine, a good friend of ours who lives just up the street. When she asked how everything was going and I shared about Gary's visit, Catherine took a deep breath and sighed. She had similar concerns and invited us to her house for a cup of coffee.

Holding Tom in my lap, Catherine began to tell me about her 45-year-old cousin with autism who had been living in an institution since he was 7 years old. She confessed that she had been watching our Tom for quite some time, wondering if there would be an opening to discuss what she knew about autism. She asked if I would be willing to talk with her Aunt Mary. Catherine was quite confident in Aunt Mary's knowledge of autism and in her advocacy for the education and care of children and adults with autism in our area. Would I want to talk to Aunt Mary? Of course!

Aunt Mary was a well-connected, well-funded parent who was eager to share all she knew of cutting edge research, understanding and practice. She was very open about her experiences with her adult son with autism who had been institutionalized most of his life. In our first meeting, Aunt Mary shared an autism checklist, newspaper articles and a recently published book, explaining how young children with autism could learn, were being educated alongside their peers and many living productive lives. She was confident that an early diagnosis could make a significant difference for Tom. She recommended an Early intervention evaluation, supports and services. While Gary and Catherine helped wake us up and made important introductions, it was Aunt Mary who planted the seeds of hope!

TOM'S THOUGHTS

My parents always told me that I was a well behaved baby. However, reading this particular chapter made me realize Gary's role in helping me reach my full potential. If he never told my parents about his concerns, I honestly doubt I would be the man I am today.

REFLECTIVE GUIDE

*Early diagnosis of children with autism is critical (Tom was 27 months)

*Parents (like us) may be initially defensive when concern is raised.

*Family/friends (like Gary & Catherine) need to speak up and be prepared for an emotional response from parents (like us).

*Seek information and resources from trustworthy organizations and trusted friends (like Aunt Mary)

1. Do you suspect that your child or student may have autism? What concerns do you have?

2. If you are a family or friend with concerns, how would you frame your approach?

3. If you are a parent, how could/did you respond to such a concern?

4. Who are your trusted friends and/or professionals with knowledge and experience with autism in young children?

CHAPTER TWO

Growing the Seeds of Hope
Early Intervention

September: Early Intervention Evaluation

The next week, in mid-September, the Island's Director of Special Education called us with contact information for Early Intervention and Children's Hospital in Boston. She explained that Tom would need two evaluations. The first would determine eligibility  for Early Intervention services. The second, by the developmental team at Children's Hospital in Boston, would evaluate and diagnose Tom. With a diagnosis of autism from a medical team Tom would then be eligible for Special Education support and services from our school district next August when he turned three. I made phone calls to get the first available appointments and marked our calendar — Children's Hospital would evaluate Tom in late November and Early Intervention would send a team to our home at the end of the month.

On a beautiful fall morning at the end of September two women from Early Intervention came to our home. The Special Educator and Occupational Therapist both interviewed us and worked through a series of tasks with Tom. The evaluation that they had planned would last for two hours was finished in less than thirty minutes after it became clear that most of what they came to do with Tom was not possible. During the evaluation Tom paced from one end of the room to the other, made no eye contact, had no language or communication skills and had no interest in any toys. On their cue, we moved to our small dining room table to review their findings. Most of what they described, my husband and I already knew, though we just didn't know the extent of delays in communication, social skill milestones and play. Based on their assessment, Tom qualified for Early Intervention services and would receive therapy weekly, in our home and at their Center-Base "off island". In our home, Tom would receive two hours of speech-language therapy and two hours of occupational therapy. At Center-Base, Tom would participate in a 2½ hour group therapy session with other children who were also diagnosed with autism. During these weekly Center Base sessions, my husband and I were invited to participate in parent therapy sessions led by a licensed psychologist. Every Friday, weather permitting, I flew with Tom (my husband Phil joined us when he could) for these group therapy sessions — kids in one room, parents in the other.

The weeks that followed were a blur of reading, talking and meeting with people from community and state-based agencies. One of these agencies was the Department of Mental Retardation (DMR). A meeting was scheduled in our home with their regional director. Based on Tom's eligibility for Early Intervention services and our low annual income we qualified for their assistance. We could (and did) request funds to purchase educational materials (books, puzzles, educational toys, etc.), therapeutic supports (bucket swing, small trampoline, etc.), conference and travel expenses (directly related to Tom's education and support), and flight vouchers (to and from Hyannis for Center Base therapy). DMR's support helped us network with other parents and professionals, and provided teaching materials we would otherwise have been unable to afford. With DMR and Early Intervention services scheduled to start for Tom in October, we began growing the seeds of hope!

October: Center Base Therapy Begins

In October, Tom began participating in Center-Based Therapy for 2½ hours once a week alongside fifteen other children between the ages of two and three years, all on the autism spectrum. With Early Intervention therapists, children used indoor and outdoor play equipment, rice tables, toys and games to improve their communication and social skills. When we arrived for our first day, Tom recognized two therapists. He separated easily from me at first, but then, realizing I was not there, began to anxiously pace. Therapists took turns calming Tom with hugs, sliding and snacks. We were encouraged to know that the therapists considered this a good first visit! Exhibit 2-1 shows the notes.

DEVELOPMENTALIST ACTIVITIES

Child's Name _Thomas Jekamoski_

Date/Time	Location/Contact	NOTES
10-25-96 9:15-11:45	CB	Good first visit for Thomas. about 45 minutes into CB – he realized mom was missing and became anxious. Was comforted by Home Visiter and able to continue to "play". – wanted to roam aimlessly, so we interrupted him with play and activities around the room. – Ate Raisens and some juice at snack time. – Outside to play – loved the outside slide. Great visit!
	P5R	M. _____ SIGNATURE - TITLE ___ Ready m.s. s.p.c.f.y. 11/10/95

Exhibit 2–1

November: Center Base Therapy Continues

Tom's second Center Base visit in November was harder than the first. He was upset when my husband and I left the room, crying on and off for the next 2½ hours. Therapists redirected him with bouncing on a therapy ball but could not prevent him from repeatedly removing his socks in order to stim. Stimming is a self-stimulatory behavior which may include repetitive movement or sounds and is part of the autism diagnosis. Stimming was a way for Tom to calm himself when he was excited or upset. Clearly upset when we left for our parent therapy session, Tom was using his socks to comfort himself.

Since he was a toddler, Tom always had something in his right hand. With object in hand next to the right side of his face, he would rapidly move his wrist back and forth quickly, frequently humming. These objects were almost always long and thin: socks, belts, a binky strap, etc. One time when we were having lunch together, I put one of his straps aside. A few minutes later, Tom was carefully tearing a paper napkin into even strips, each about an inch wide. As I continued to watch, he bunched them together, wrapped his little hand around the center, lifted it up the side of his eye, and began stimming in delight. I was amazed at his precision and his problem solving skills. He wanted something to stim with. I had taken his strap away. He made a strap from a paper napkin nearby. Problem solved.

Center Based visits continued for the next seven months. These early session notes provided a baseline of Tom's emotions as well as his need for much prompting to engage with others. With no communication system, Tom could not express himself or even make a simple request. My heart went out to my son, knowing how scary and hard all of this must have been. The only comfort I had was the belief that pushing through all of this and teaching him to engage and communicate, would help his life. We were on a mission! Not knowing his full potential, we believed that Tom was capable of more than he was able to show. So, Exhibit 2-2 shows the notes from the second Center Base session.

Private School Visits

In early November, we heard of nearby private schools successfully educating children with autism. We narrowed the list down to three schools within driving distance- two schools outside Boston and one school on the Cape- all of them reporting progress teaching the very young. Our plan was to see their programs in action and advocate to staff a similar program in our local school. We were grateful that the Department of Mental Retardation funded these visits.

We started by touring The New England Center for Autism, then The Higashi School and finished with The May Institute. All three schools were most impressive! They used two different belief systems to frame their educational programs. The Higashi school based their approach on a methodology called Daily Life Therapy while The New England Center and May Institute were grounded in Applied Behavioral Analysis. I had read articles on both approaches and was very interested to see their school based implementation.

What we found most interesting were the similarities. All three were intensive 30-40 hours per week for children ages 3-5. All three used a collaborative approach with multi-disciplinary teams, focused on individualized instruction, and taught specific skills to master as part of explicit curriculums in communication, fine motor, social skills and academics. All three schools produced data showing impressive results. We came

DEVELOPMENTALIST ACTIVITIES

Child's Name _Thomas Jevanowski_

Date/Time	Location/ Contact	NOTES
11/1/96 9:15–11:45	CB	Thomas sad when mom + dad left. Needed his socks for comfort. Cried off + on throughout morning. Explored the room. Checking out the areas, watching fleetingly, at cracked corn + bead table. Was able to get Thomas on the therapy ball a couple of times – didn't mind the bouncing. Very interested in the computer. Would watch as Sesame Street Characters showed up + with help (hesitantly) pushed buttons to change pictures. Snacktime – ate ritz bits, ate a few pcs of peaches ~~drank + ~~ juice. Got his shoes + socks on for outside. outside – Checked out wild animals, climbed up + down ramp.
	PJR	SIGNATURE - TITLE ____ m.s. SLP CFY 11/10/95

Exhibit 2–2

back from these schools, inspired that we could provide something similar for Tom on the island. Following his upcoming diagnostic evaluation, we would meet with Early Intervention to advocate for their approval and funding.

The Evaluation

Late November came quickly and it was time for Tom's evaluation appointment at Boston Children's Hospital. Our family left the day before, and stayed overnight with good friends, which was tremendously comforting. Early the next morning, Philip drove Tom and me to the hospital, while he spent the day in the city with Patrick.

The evaluation took the better part of a day. It began with an interview asking general questions about pregnancy, birth, followed by developmental questions about Tom's behavior, talking and play. At the time, Tom was twenty-seven months old and did not talk. Although there had been some vocalizations around twelve months, now there was nothing. When he paced, usually on his toes, he would hum, flap and body tense, but no babbling. There was no eye contact and there was no interest in toys, play or others—except for me. I explained to them how he walked at ten months, slept through the night and nursed well. They wrote everything down.

After my interview, many professionals took turns evaluating Tom's cognitive, social emotional, communication, fine motor and gross motor skills. Some of these sessions were short because Tom was unable to follow directions and had little interest in engaging with anyone except me. Following the last test, each specialist met with me to review their findings. In their report, the developmental psychologists found "that his lack of attention and self-directiveness limited the testing. He engaged in no social play. Our report is therefore based on behavioral observations and parental reports. He exhibited limited problem solving skills." Physical therapists "found that his self-directed behavior limited the testing. Overall his fine and gross motor skills were in the fifteen-to-seventeen month range. In summary, Thomas is a two-year three-month-old boy who meets the criteria for autism. He is currently receiving occupational and speech therapy. He is scheduled to start a behavioral program in the next two weeks. Recommendations: Obtain an EEG (rule out fragile X). Continue Early Intervention services (occupational, speech, play and behavioral therapies). At three years of age, he should attend a full day, full year, behavior oriented program with occupational and speech therapies at school. Follow- up for psychological evaluation in 6 months. Parental referral for support group." (Boston Children's Hospital DMC Clinic, November 26, 1996).

We were grateful for their reports and ready to move forward. With a diagnosis of autism, we could now approach Early Intervention to fund a consultant to help us implement an intensive ABA home-based program. Tom's overall cognitive functioning was estimated in the six to nine-month range — there was a lot of work to be done.

With help from a consultant at The May Center in Chatham, we had outlined an educational plan for Tom based on the principals of applied behavioral analysis (ABA). I then met with Early Intervention to seek funding for this ABA home plan. The Director of Early Intervention looked at me in disbelief! She was adamant that what I was proposing was developmentally inappropriate for a child Tom's age and could actually be harmful. She further stated that this type of a program had never been requested before, that they had no relationship with The May Center, and she reminded me of all the other programs and therapies other families were using. I listened politely and responded that we believed that this

ABA Home-based program, with an experienced consultant, was what our son Tom needed. I cited research articles and books of similar programs which shared data proving the progress made by children who were only two to three years old. When she saw that I was resolute, the Director conceded, and had me sign a funding requisition form for our ABA program.

I remember calling my parents to share the news. Both of my parents were in the medical field—my dad a physician specializing in adult internal medicine, and my mom a retired nurse. I told them all about the evaluation results and diagnosis of autism. I shared the hope we felt. I also shared that our home program would be led by a prominent consultant and Tom would have fifteen to twenty hours every week of 1:1 therapy and teaching sessions. My parents were impressed with everything we knew and praised our optimism. Many years later, my mom shared with me that when my dad got off the phone, he wept. It was only the second time she had ever seen him cry.

December: First Home-Based Program Meeting

In December, with Tom's diagnosis of autism official and funding now approved, we were excited about having a consultant and therapists in our home program. With funding from Early Intervention, we were able to hire two certified teachers, Andrea and Kathy. both willing to be trained by our consultant. Andrea would commute from the mainland, while Kathy lived just down the street.

Tom's home-based program would now include fifteen to twenty hours per week of 1:1 sessions based on the principals of applied behavioral analysis under Marilyn's direction. Seven days a week, for two to three hours a day, Tom would work with an ABA therapist, an Early Intervention therapist, or go to Center Base group therapy. Marilyn would come to our home once or twice a week, as her schedule and weather permitted. In addition to teaching Tom, she would also train therapists and our family, provide reports summarizing data collection/analysis and make recommendations for the following week. Tom would continue weekly speech-language and occupational therapy. One of our Early Intervention therapists was upfront about being philosophically opposed to ABA. We respected her expertise. She was animated, engaging and willing to work with Tom on his weekly ABA goals. She continued and we were happy she did! Although we scheduled fifteen to twenty hours of 1:1 sessions per week, we actually averaged about ten to fifteen hours a week, mostly on account of the weather.

The first meeting with our consultant and lead teacher in early December was very productive. Marilyn, Andrea and I reviewed Tom's recent evaluation, discussed priorities and listed thirteen achievable goals. Marilyn then explained how we would be tracking Tom's progress on each of these goals for each teaching session. Together, we would focus on improving Tom's ability to attend, communicate and play. We would also use these same techniques to reduce head banging, crying, tantrums and self-stimulatory behaviors (i.e. strap flipping, hand flapping, pacing, etc.).

Data would guide all decisions in helping Tom master his goals. Marilyn talked us through the basics of data analysis. For each goal, in every teaching session, we were to take data, review data and make all decisions based on our individual and collective data reviews. When Tom was making progress on a goal, we would continue our teaching program. If he was not making progress or his progress was slow, as a team, we would discuss and make changes to our teaching and/or materials. This daily and weekly data analysis process with Marilyn continued for the duration of our eight-month home program.

We learned about applied behavioral analysis and how we would teach Tom using a discrete trial teaching model. Throughout our first meeting, Marilyn would demonstrate these teaching techniques with Tom. Andrea and I also took turns practicing. Marilyn was very clear in her demonstrations and in the form she shared with us for keeping data for every teaching goal in every teaching session. Marilyn would begin her first teaching session with Tom, the following week.

Exhibits 2-3 and 2-4 contain the notes from our first meeting and the six-month goals we set for Tom that day.

First Teaching Session

Tom's first session with Marilyn was in late December and focused on attending (eye contact and sitting in a chair), communication (instruction following, pointing and picture identification), and motor imitation/social/play (mimicking another person's movements, e.g. stack blocks, clap hands, wave bye-bye, etc.). Everything in this first session was new to Tom, except for my presence. I joined Marilyn for parts of the first few sessions to help Tom transition and also to learn. But when I was not there, Tom screamed and cried—a lot! This was so hard to listen to, so sometimes I had to go for a walk. I wanted so badly to comfort him.

Tom was not the only one learning! Marilyn taught me, my husband, Patrick, therapists and many of our extended family and friends. She taught us how to redirect Tom's protests and instead of reacting, teach him to follow directions and communicate. We learned to be direct, using the same, simple phrases when speaking to Tom. We learned to follow through with physical prompting if we asked him to do something and he did not. We

The May Institute, Inc.
May Center for Child Development
100 Seaview Street
P.O. Box 708
Chatham, MA 02633
(508) 945-1147

Home-Based Consultation

Child: Tommy Jackanawski
Date: 12/7/96
Time: 11:30 am - 3:00pm

Elizabeth, Andrea, and I met and talked about 6-month goals and objectives for Tommy primarily in the areas of attending, communication, and play skills. The priority skills, program steps, and data collection will be listed on an individual form. This form will be revised and updated as needed throughout the home-based program. Data collection will be an ongoing assessment of progress and we will record data for each skill area. The first form revision is included with this case note.

We then discussed applied behavior analysis, the discrete trial teaching model and task analysis. An outline of what we reviewed is attached to this case note. Throughout the session I took opportunities to interact with Tommy to explain prompting techniques. I also guided Elizabeth through a few incidental teaching situations with Tommy.

The first teaching session with Tommy is scheduled for December 14th.

Marilyn Murray   12/9/96
Marilyn S. Murray, M. A.   Date
Consultant

Exhibit 2–3

helped Tom understand what we were asking by showing, not just telling him. We still let him hum and flap with his favorite straps but now, after a short time, we would call him back to engage with us in an activity like a puzzle or a book or a swing.

Tom also loved to jump on the trampoline. These were great ways to re-engage him if he was becoming tired or bored. When not in sessions, keeping Tom engaged in purposeful and playful activities during his waking hours became our family's priority. Patrick was happy to join us and loved pushing Tom in our kitchen swing.

Exhibits 2-5a and 2-5b are our first teaching session notes.

January: Parent Support Group, Center Base

Every Friday, Philip and I flew over to the mainland for Tom's Center-Based

The May Institute, Inc.
May Center for Child Development
100 Sea View Street
P.0. Box 708
Chatham, MA 02633
(508) 945-1147

Home-Based Consultation
Six month Goals and Objectives

Child: Tommy Jekanowski
Date: 12/96

Tommy will improve attending, communication, and play skills for 80% of
the given opportunities. Tommy will reduce head banging,
crying/tantrums, and self-stimulatory behaviors.

1. Tommy will respond with eye contact when his name is called or when
"look" or "look at me" is said to him when he is engaged in an activity.

2. Tommy will sit at the table engaged in an activity for up to 5 minutes.

3. Tommy will follow 6 one-step instructions.

4. Tommy will spontaneously point to a desired item when given a choice.

5. Tommy will verbally approximate 3 sounds/words.

6. Tommy will learn to match 3 different objects to an identical object.

7. Tommy will imitate 7 gross and fine motor skills.

8. Tommy will receptively identify 3 objects/items.

9. Tommy will sit at the table and use his spoon to feed himself.

10. Tommy will engage in songs, story books, turntaking, and interactive play
with an adult for 5 minutes without exhibiting self-stimulatory behavior.

11. Tommy will request by exchanging a Mayer-Johnson icon for a desired
item.

12. Tommy will walk up and down stairs with one hand held.

13. Tommy will decrease head banging, crying/tantrum and self-stimulatory
behaviors.

Exhibit 2–4

therapy and our parent support sessions and (as usual)
kids in one room, parents in the other. Parent to parent, these discussions connected and comforted us. Our
new friends understood what we said and even what
we didn't say or couldn't put into words. We cheered
for our childrens' small victories, cried over setbacks
and sometimes laughed at situations others might have
thought odd or inappropriate.

Along with our growing friendships at Center Base, Tom's January data showed that he was making progress. Tom was beginning to make eye contact and point in our home based sessions. He was beginning to put blocks into a container, stack blocks, and put one piece into a puzzle. Tom was starting to "play" with a toy car and wave bye bye. While engaging in or attempting these tasks, Tom did not cry, tantrum or head bang!

Of the fifteen children in Center Base, Tom was the most significantly delayed in communication and cognitive skills. While many parents were

---

The May Institute, Inc.
May Center for Child Development
100 Sea View Street
P.O. Box 708
Chatham, MA 02633
(508) 945-1147

Home-Based Consultation

Child: Tommy Jeckanawski
Date: 12/21/96
Time: 9:30 am - 12:30pm

Elizabeth and I both ran the session today with Tommy. He was cooperative and tried new materials when they were presented, but only for very short durations (10 to 20 seconds). When he was engaged with singing a song, especially with his mother, he attended for longer durations (up to one minute). Tommy makes excellent eye contact when you sing preferred songs (John Jacob Jingle ...., and The Wheels on the Bus) with him. However, when you request him to look at you, he does not always do so.

During the second half of this session he wanted to take off his socks. He then became very fixated on wanting to wave the sock in a self-stimulatory manner. When the sock was removed from him, he was very upset and persistent in trying to find it. Because it was interfering with Tommy attending and learning new skills, we removed the sock from the room.

The following is behavior data from the session: (Please refer to data sheet for definition of each behavior)
Head banging - frequency during the first half of the session was 7; and during the second half was 4.
Crying/tantrum - frequency during the first half of the session was 1; and during the second half was 5.

The following is program data from the session: (Please refer to the attached program sheet for a description of each individual program and the current step that Tommy is learning).
Attending skills:
Eye contact - step 1; averaged 20%
Sitting in a chair at the table - step 2; averaged 40%

Communication skills:
Instruction following - step 2; averaged 0%
Pointing - step 1; 20% (2 trials without resistance but with physical prompts)
Picture Identification/Exchange - step 1; 0% (all trials are physical prompts)

Exhibit 2–5a

Imitation/Social/Play skills:
Motor imitation - step 1 is learning 7 motor skills:
       1. stacking blocks - no data
       2. push car back and forth - averaged 0%
       3. blocks in container - averaged 60%
       4. put lid on container - averaged 0%
       5. clap hands - averaged 0%
       6. wave bye-bye - averaged 0%
       7. puts one piece in puzzle - no data

Based on this session I would recommend removing any item/toy that interferes with Tommy attending to either you or to the task he is asked to complete.

Marilyn Murray
_____
Marilyn S. Murray, M. A.
Consultant

12/22/99
Date

Exhibit 2–5b

focusing on diet, medication, play therapy and sensory approaches, we were focused on education. By mid-January, Tom was beginning to show progress with Applied Behavioral Analysis. Some wanted to know more about our home program. We explained that having a consultant was key. Some decided to try ABA while others held fast to their own therapies.

Exhibit 2-6 represents Consultant Marilyn Murray's notes from an early January home-based session.

Teaching Feedback from our Consultant

In addition to teaching Tom, Marilyn gave feedback on our teaching, in person and after reviewing videotaped sessions. In her review of one of Andrea's early sessions, she praised Tom's progress in sitting and simple motor imitation. Then she listed ways to improve what she saw in the video. The first suggestion was something for all of us to work on: when asking Tom to do something, don't repeat following the instruction. Either reinforce with praise like "go play" or prompt him to the correct response. Tom was learning language through our consistent responses. It was essential that our words and phrases were clearly connected to concrete objects and actions. This word means this and that word/phrase means that. All of our teaching needed to be explicit, concrete, consistent and repeated for Tom to learn.

Marilyn's second suggestion reminded us to interrupt Tom's current practice of "point and grab." We needed to teach Tom that after pointing to a desired item, to wait by putting his hands in his lap. Only after his hands were in his lap for a few seconds were we to give him the desired item.

The May Institute, Inc.
May Center for Child Development
100 Sea View Street
P.O. Box 708
Chatham, MA 02633
(508) 945-1147
Home-Based Consultation

Child: Tommy Jeskanawski
Date: 1/4/97
Time: 9:30 AM - 12:30 PM

Elizabeth and I took turns teaching during this session. We were able to continuously engage Tommy for 1 hour and 25 minutes. After a 15 minute break downstairs I ran an individual session for 40 minutes. Lunch time followed and Tommy easily transitioned to the table to sit down for lunch.

Behavior data:
Head banging - no occurrences
Crying/tantrum - no occurrences
Self-stimulation - no occurrences

Program data:
Attending skills:
Eye contact - step 1; averaged 80%
Sitting in a chair at the table - step 3; averaged 90% (next session, move to step 4)

Communication skills:
Instruction following - step 2; averaged 50%
Pointing - step 1; 60% (Tommy is allowing partial prompting and there is no resistance)
Picture Identification/Exchange - step 1; 0% (all trials are physical prompts)
Verbal imitation - step 1; averaged 0% (program added 12/28/96)

Imitation/Social/Play skills:
Motor imitation - step 1 is learning 7 motor skills:
     1. stacking blocks - averaged 60%
     2. push car back and forth - averaged 80%
     3. blocks in container - averaged 100% (achieved)
     4. put lid on container - averaged 20%
     5. clap hands - averaged 0%
     6. wave bye-bye - averaged 60%
     7. puts one piece in puzzle (without assistance) - averaged 80%

Marilyn S. Murray   _1/6/97_
Marilyn S. Murray, M. A.   Date
Consultant

Exhibit 2–6

Teaching this way was effective. Soon after we made this change, Tom stopped grabbing and he learned to wait.

With her third, fourth and fifth suggestions, Marilyn reminded us to always pair a verbal instruction with a task, for example, to make sure Tom picked up a picture before giving him (not letting him grab) the item, and continuing to comment while Tom engaged in "play time." Exhibit 2-7 shows Marilyn's suggestions based on Andrea's videotaped session.

May Center for Child Development
100 Sea View Street
P.O. Box 708
Chatham, MA 02633
(508) 945-1147

Evaluation of 1/5/97 session
Child: Tommy Jekanowski
Date: 1/14/97
Therapist: Andrea

Overall, during the session Tommy demonstrated progress in sitting in his chair at the table, completing various motor tasks, and readily coming over to the table. You exhibited good fading of prompting techniques and this has promoted development of Tommy's problem solving skills on learned tasks. Your reinforcement is beginning to vary more and this will help Tommy to discriminate between when he has completed a task with no prompting ("yeahs", hugs, kisses, tickles, etc.) versus being cooperative and allowing you to prompt him ("go play").

The following are some suggestions to practice in your sessions with Tommy:

1. If you give Tommy an instruction or use a point prompt (i.e., point to chair for Tommy to sit down) then follow through by having him comply. If he wants to stand to complete a task and it's okay with you, then tell him he can stand but only after he sits down. Try to say instruction once, then either reinforce Tommy's correct response or prompt correct response.

2. After pointing to a desired item, have Tommy put his hands down and then you give him the item. We want to interrupt the point-and-grab chain that he is doing.

3. Remember the discrete trial format. In many of the trials there is not a discriminative stimulus given, other than "sit down". I think Tommy may be coming to the table looking at the task and completing it. You are reinforcing him for completion which is good, however, receptively he did not have to listen and pair an instruction that was related to the task.

4. During picture exchange, it is great how you increased your distance to the opposite side of the table. If Tommy reaches for item before picking up the picture, have him start again by putting his hands down. Use a full physical prompt to correct him, then try again before giving him the item.

5. Continue to comment while Tommy is engaged in play time. Continue with the interactive play, too. It was fun to watch "Head, shoulders ..." and to see Tommy initiating. Increasing the duration of time is a good goal as well as working on eye contact, "more", body parts, etc. That interaction was around 4 minutes.

We can review any of these suggestions, Andrea, over the telephone or in person. If you have any other questions, please don't hesitate to call me. It is wonderful to see Tommy's progress in the six weeks since we first began.

Exhibit 2–7

February: Home Program Progress

Tom was progressing on all goals by February, except verbal imitation. By the tenth week of home based sessions, eye contact with therapists was improving as was the time he was sitting in his chair during sessions. Tom  was beginning to follow simple instructions, to point, identify a few objects and use pictures to communicate.

In February, we started teaching body parts and toilet training. When toileting was first introduced, Tom cried the entire time until he was returned to his bedroom where he could play. Even this tearful toileting session in February showed progress. Tom calmed down when he was returned to play. Now, because of these sessions, he actually had toys he would play with and books to look at. This was huge!

The only goal on which Tom was not progressing was verbal imitation. We all believed his language would be emerging by this time, but it was not. Sometimes when he was sleeping, I wondered whether he would ever talk and, if he did, what his voice would sound like...

Exhibit 2-8a-b below shows notes from an early February home-based session.

March: Rate of Learning Increases

The pace of Tom's learning in our home sessions was increasing in March. By the fourteenth week, he had mastered a few goals, made progress in others (except verbal imitation), and was working on new goals in self-care. Tom was now using a picture to request something he wanted, feeding himself with a spoon (independently), and walking up and down the stairs with one hand held.

Tom was making progress with eye contact when his name was called, engaging and staying engaged in an activity, following 1-step instructions, spontaneously pointing to a desired item, imitating gestures, receptively identifying objects, engaging in an activity without self-stimulating behaviors (humming, flapping, etc.), and decreasing the frequency of tantrums.

New goals for Tom introduced this month included undressing, sitting on the toilet, receptive identification of body parts and drinking from a cup without a lid. Exhibits 2-9a-b show the 3-month progress notes.

The May Institute, Inc.
May Center for Child Development
100 Sea View Street
P.0. Box 708
Chatham, MA 02633
(508) 945-1147

Home-Based Consultation

Child: Tommy Jekanowski
Date: 2/1/97
Time: 9:35 - 11:05 AM
         11:15 AM - 12:00 PM

The frequency of Tommy asking for help is increasing. He is requesting
assistance by taking your hand to help him. Over the past few sessions I have
shaped his hands to sign "help" while modeling the word. Both sessions
went well with eye contact improving during natural interactions. During
toilet training Tommy cried throughout the entire routine. After we went
back to his bedroom to continue the session he stopped the crying and became
involved in playing with different toys. During the second session, he began
requesting food continuously between 11:45 and 12. There were opportunities
for 15 trials of the picture exchange for the item Tommy was requesting. He
spontaneously came from across the room to where I was and handed me the
picture that he had taken off of the communication book in exchange for the
item he wanted. He was requesting pretzel, raisin, and juice.

Behavior data (average of both sessions): (refer to data sheet for definition of behaviors)
Head banging - 5
Crying/tantrum - 1
Self-stimulation - 0

Attending skills: (refer to program sheet for task analysis)
Eye contact - step 3; averaged 80%
Sitting in a chair at the table - step 5; averaged 80%

Communication skills:
Instruction following - step 3; averaged 30%
Pointing - step 2; 20%
Picture Identification/Exchange - step 4; 70%
Verbal imitation - step 1a; averaged 0% (program revised)
Object Identification - step 4; averaged 60%
Protest: step 1; averaged 88%
Waiting: step 1; averaged 50%
Receptive Identification of Body Parts: step 1; averaged 0%

Exhibit 2–8a

Enjoying Center Base

Tom's Center Base sessions were going very well. Tom was separating
from me easily, using sign language and pictures to communicate, enjoying an increasing variety of play activities and, decreasing his need for
prompts by the end of March. One of Tom's favorite activities at Center
Base was blowing and popping bubbles. We made sure to always have several bottles at home. We used them during his home sessions and anytime

Imitation/Social/Play skills:
Motor imitation - Step 1 is seven motor skills: Tommy has learned four out of the seven motor skills. We will continue to work on clap hands, wave bye, and lids on containers incidentally.

Step 2: This session four new motor imitations were introduced. They are: tap table, arms up, stomp feet, and Indian noises. Data was 0%.

Self help skills:
Spoon use: Tommy can complete the entire chain. He sometimes has difficulty scooping and continues to prefer eating with his fingers. His parents continue to practice spoon use with highly preferred foods like ice cream.

Undressing:
Shoes, socks, and pants: 9 prompts were needed for Tommy to take off his shoes, socks, and pants.

Toilet Training:
Tommy cried throughout the sequence of stepping up on the stool, sitting down on the toilet, standing up, and stepping down from the stool. He sat for 5 seconds.

In summary, all programs are progressing with the exception of verbal imitation. We will continue to model the sign to accompany the word. Teaching discrimination with the picture exchange is the next step. We will also begin to generalize to one picture on the board that Tommy's parents have put on the wall in the kitchen.

Marilyn Murray
Marilyn S. Murray, M. A.
Consultant

2/3/97
Date

Exhibit 2–8b

during the day, just for fun! Of all the American Language signs we used with Tom, "bubbles" was one of the most popular. Only "Mama" and "cookies" were used more.

Tom began to really enjoy center base sessions! I think there were several reasons for this. He was becoming familiar with the other children and therapists, as well as the "routine". He knew what equipment and toys were inside and outside. No longer scared or anxious, Tom was now participating in many activities such as the seesaw platform, bubble blowing, and more importantly, bubble popping, and a challenging obstacle course made up of ins, outs, ups and down-unders. Tom especially enjoyed finding objects buried in the rice table. In fact, Tom became so comfortable that during one session in March he actually fell asleep on one of the therapist's shoulders.

Exhibit 2-10 contains the notes.

The May Institute, Inc.
May Center for Child Development
100 Sea View Street
P.O. Box 708
Chatham, MA 02633
(508) 945-1147

Home-Based Consultation
Three Month Progress Note

Child: Tommy Jekanowski
Date: 3/17/97

The following are program objectives that were introduced December 14th. Of the 13 objectives being addressed: 3 have been achieved; 8 are progressing; 1 is not progressing; and 1 has not been introduced. Current performance levels on each goal are indicated below.

Program Goal: Tommy will improve attending, communication, and play skills for 80% of the given opportunities. Tommy will reduce head banging, crying/tantrums, and self-stimulatory behaviors 80% from baseline.

Objectives:
1. Tommy will respond with eye contact when his name is called or when "look" or "look at me" is said to him when he is engaged in an activity. (progressing; currently in generalization step and averaging 65%).

2. Tommy will sit at the table engaged in an activity for up to 5 minutes. (progressing; has achieved sitting at the table with an activity for 3 minutes; has on occasion demonstrated being able to stay with a preferred activity for up to 7 minutes.)

3. Tommy will follow 6 one-step instructions. (progressing; has achieved 4 one step instructions, "sit down", "come here", "give it to me", and "stand up"; currently on step 5, "bring it to the table". The instruction "hands down" was not progressing so it was discontinued; it continues to be practiced incidentally.)

4. Tommy will spontaneously point to a desired item when given a choice. (progressing; partial prompt needed to shape a point response)

5. Tommy will verbally approximate 3 sounds/words. (not progressing; vocal play is increasing.)

Exhibit 2–9a

April & May: Autism Service Plan Advocacy

I had an opportunity to reflect and offer feedback on service plans for young children with autism to the state agency funding Early Intervention. Too late in receiving the notice to attend the meeting in person, I sent a letter responding to their four questions.

The first question asked parents to describe what were considered the essential components of services to children with Pervasive Developmental Disorder (PDD). PDD was, and still is, considered by many

Tommy Jekanowski   Three Month Progress Note
Page 2

6. Tommy will learn to match 3 different objects to an identical object.
   (not introduced; will be introduced this month)

7. Tommy will imitate 7 gross and fine motor skills.
   (progressing; has learned motor movements with objects and continues to
   work on imitating motor movements without objects)

8. Tommy will receptively identify 3 objects/items.
   (progressing; currently identifying one object from field of 2 items and
   averaging 50%)

9. Tommy will sit at the table and use his spoon to feed himself. (achieved)

10. Tommy will engage in songs, story books, turn taking, and interactive play
    with an adult for 5 minutes without exhibiting self-stimulatory behavior.
    (progressing; currently averaging 3 minutes; has been engaged for up to 7
    minutes)

11. Tommy will request by exchanging a Mayer-Johnson icon for a desired
    item. (achieved; currently on step 5 and working on discrimination
    between a preferred and non-preferred item)

12. Tommy will walk up and down stairs with one hand held. (achieved)

13. Tommy will decrease head banging, crying/tantrum and self-stimulatory
    behaviors from baseline levels. (progressing)

The three objectives that have been achieved continue to be practiced so
Tommy maintains these skills. New objectives that have been introduced
are: Undressing, Sitting on the toilet, Receptive identification of body parts,
and Drinking from a cup without a lid. Vocal and motor imitation trials will
be increased during sessions.

Marilyn S. Murray   3/17/97
Marilyn S. Murray, M. A.   Date
Behavioral Consultant

Exhibit 2–9b

clinicians to be synonymous with Autism Spectrum Disorder (ASD). I described our 15-20 hour 1:1 home based program and the essential role of
a consultant. Our consultant trained all therapists and our family, led us
in setting functional, developmental goals, set the steps to achieve these
goals, and helped provide teaching materials. We believed the intensity
and type of our home based program was the reason for Tom's progress
to date. When Tom began early intervention, he was non-verbal, had no
play skills, perseverated with his strap or string-like object most of the
day, and had frequent tantrums. After five months of early intervention

DEVELOPMENTALIST ACTIVITIES

Child's Name __Thomas Jekam__

Time	Location/Contact	NOTES
3/28/97 9:15-1:45	CB	Thomas had a good day in centerbase. He loves the platform + the bubbles. Great signing for "more bubbles". He participated in the obstacle course with very little prompting. Lots of smiles. At snack he ate crackers, pretzels + his juice. Outside we played in the seed sensory the slides + fell asleep on P.J.'s shoulder after exhausting himself in the fresh air + sunshine. Good day!

SIGNATURE - TITLE _____ Spec Ed CEIS

PJR   BW

Exhibit 2–10

services, Tom was still non-verbal but now could use five different signs, played with 15 toys and when engaged in tasks, music, or play could go for periods of time without his strap.

The second question asked about models of service delivery that were applicable to various parts of the state. I really vented in my response to this question. We were living on an island 30 miles out to sea and because of the weather (wind and fog), about half of Tom's service providers cancelled on any given week. My suggestions here were quite strong and very clear: there was a great need for Early Intervention therapists to reside in one or both of our state's islands to more consistently provide services to the children living there. Early Intervention provided a program model of 2 home visits per week (two hours with an early intervention staffer and two hours with an occupational therapist) and a weekly 2½-hour center-based group session along with a concurrent parent therapy session. Of the 15 families we saw weekly at Center Base, 3 of us were using an intensive, ABA, home-based program, 3 were using a popular play therapy "LCDC", 3 were using the standard early intervention program, and 6 were unknown.

The third question asked for input on how specialty service providers such as The May Center, LCDC Play Therapy (The Miller Method), etc. and early intervention could work together to provide a range of services to families.

My response also addressed the fourth question which asked for input on reimbursement because, in my mind, these questions overlapped, so I answered them together. I suggested when evaluating potential service providers that they also consider experience and commitment. A sliding fee schedule, based on education, certification and experience was another suggestion. In addition, because there were delays for some of our therapists starting because of paperwork processing, I suggested a more streamlined process.

I was pleased when I received a positive response to my letter from the coordinator about three weeks later. I enjoyed meeting her in person at another parent input meeting about a week after I had written my letter, and was able to thank her for seeking our input. Holding on to hope, I prayed that our individual and collective feedback would help improve their systems.... Exhibits 2-11a-c displays my feedback.

June: 6 Month Goals Achieved!

June marked the sixth month of our home-based sessions. We were thrilled with Tom's progress! He had achieved 12 of his 13 goals! Tom now made

eye contact when his name was called, sat at a table engaged in an activity for at least five minutes, followed six different 1-step directions, spontaneously pointed to a desired item, matched six objects to an identical object, and imitated thirteen motor movements.

Tom also receptively identified three objects/items, used his spoon to feed himself, engaged in songs and other tasks for five minutes without stimming, requested an item using a picture, and was decreasing head banging and tantrums.

Still no progress with vocal imitation and he continued to protest new materials.

May 2,1997

Tracy Osbahr
Coordinator of Specialty Sevices
Department of Public Health
Western Regional Health Office
23 Service Center
Northhampton, MA 01060

Philip and Elizabeth Jekanowski
3 Pond Road
Nantucket, MA 02554

Dear Ms. Osbahr;
As a parent of a 2 1/2 year old autistic boy who has been receiving services from
Cape Cod Early Intervention for about 5 months, I would like to respond to the
letter you sent on March 24 regarding a meeting to discuss service plans for children
0-3 yrs. with PDD spectrum. By the time we received your invitation, it was too late
to make plans to come, but I would now like to take the time to respond to the
following questions proposed in your letter.

There is so much more information that should be made available to parents with a
child newly diagnosed with PDD. Our weekly parent group has been brainstorming
as to what we would like to see CCEI offer new parents about the PDD spectrum,
where to go for diagnostic evaluations, the scope of future possibilities for their
child, forms of tried and tested interventions currently being used with the
population at large, names and contact information for all the public servie agencies
that one would now qualify for, and a phone list of chosen parents whose children
have recently "graduated"from CCEI and have valuable experience and empathy to
share.

QUESTION#1:
.
*I can only speak from my experience with my child and from what I have shared with
other parents using the same type of program.*

What are the essential components of services to children with PDD?

*20-30 hours of home based, one on one teaching that incorporates and allows a
variety of activities and stimulation. This program is also proved most effective
when the parent(s)are closely monitoring teaching techniques and material to carry
over into the rest of the day in order to facilitate generalization.

Exhibit 2–11a

Tom's rate of learning was increasing. He was now able to demonstrate what he knew across teachers, sessions and even different materials. Tom was making progress sitting on the toilet, drinking from a cup,
matching colors and he was able to receptively identify five body parts.
Tom now used four signs appropriately—mama, cookie, help, and eat.
    Exhibits 2-12a and b show the 6-month progress notes.

*Must have a qualified pogram leader whose job it is to design functional teaching programs, their content and pace; to train all other teachers if need be; to work closely with the parents in order to brainstorm together about the ever changing needs of the child and his/her family.
*We personally feel that our son would not have made the progress that he has if we had not been using ABA teaching techniques in a daily, all out intensive home program.

My son Tommy is non-verbal, had no play skills, perseverated throughout the day on strings or string-like material, and postured frequently(we always called it bodytensing before we knew the technical term).
After 3 1/2 months of primarily an intensive(aiming at about 20 hrs/week) ABA home-based program, with 4 teachers and myself, our son now uses 5 signs(American Sign Language) to communicate, can and will play with some prompting with about 15 toys, can go for longer parts of the day without seeking his "string", enjoys looking through books, and we have found regular deep pressured "hugs" and rough housing throughout the day are especially helpful in reducing his need to posture or engage in self-stimulartory behavoir.

QUESTION #2:
What models of service delivery are applicable to various parts of the state?

We have been particularly frustrated in the lack of consistency in service from our teachers and therpists due primarily to transportation problems due to our residence being Nantucket Island. We have only been receiving about half of the services for any given week that are on our FSP. We are currently training on-island people to become part of our teaching team. The locations of Nantucket and Martha's Vinyard should be considered as especially challenging location to service young autistic children, and current CCEI staff and Specilty Service Providers are unable to meet this growing need. There needs to be more professionally trained people in ABA and the standard CCEI trained model residing in these locations.

Cape Cod Early Intervention made an initial evaluation in our home and began offering us services the next week. They offered us their standard model of intervention which consists of 2- two hour visits, one by an CCEI staff(ours has much experience with PDD) and the other by an Occupational Therapist with Sensory Intergration Certification. They also were able to offer us a PDD spectrum therapy group that paralleled a parent support group once a week for 2 1/2 hours There are currently 15 children with the PDD spectrum at CCEI, and of those that regularly attend our weekly parent group, here is the breakdown of program choice and place of teacher origin:
3 parents are currently utilizing The May Center in Chatham for an intensive ABA home-based program
3 parents are currently traveling to LCDC in Falmouth(?) for 3 one hour sesssions/week supplimented by their incidental home intervention

Exhibit 2–11b

3 parents are operating on the standard CCEI model of intervention, consisting of 4 hours of home based visits, and participation in the weekly therapy group and parent support group
6 parents program's unknown
**The weekly parent group has been a tremendous help to our family and has helped in areas where nothing else could.

QUESTION #3:
How could Specialty Service Providers and existing Early Intervention Programs work together to provide a range of services to families?

**Need to value experience and committement equal to if not more important than education in evaluation potential service providers.
*Specialty Service Providers should be contracted directly to defray the cost of paperwork and help alleviate the delay of services because of the current system of billing.
*Staff should be compensated on a sliding scale for services rendered based on their education and experience with PDD
*CCEI needs to expand their staff base, current resources have forced parents who would have preferred CCEI staff for services, to utilize "Specialty" groups

CCEI has done this coordinating very well. They have remained available to parents and Specialty Serivce Providers in a highly consistent maner - they care!

QUESTION #4:
What models of reimbursement have applicability in Massachusetts?

(I feel that I have already responded to this question in #3)

We have been very alarmed at the current ignorance and misinformation that still permeates our society regarding the diagnosis of autism/PDD-NOS. This quote is from a Monday March 31 article in the Boston Globe :
"moderate developemental delays include those...with Pervasive Developemental Disorder, an autism-like syndrome where children don't make eye contact,fail to speak, or have difficulaty with even the most basic motor skills."
*PDD of itself is not a diagnostic category! and it is not "autistic-like", it is!

Thank you for taking the time to read this letter and consider its contents. We have been very happy with the services CCEI have provided and coordinated for our son Tommy.

Sincerely,

Elizabeth Jekanowski
Elizabeth Jekanowski

Exhibit 2–11c

The May Institute, Inc.
May Center for Child Development
100 Sea View Street
P.O. Box 708
Chatham, MA 02633
(508) 945-1147

Home-Based Consultation
Six Month Progress Note

Child: Tommy Jekanowski
Date: 6/23/97

The following are program objectives that were introduced December 14,
1996. Of the 13 objectives addressed: 12 have been achieved and 1 is not
progressing. The objective not progressing is verbal approximation. Current
performance levels on each goal are indicated below.

Program Goal: Tommy will improve attending, communication, and play
skills for 80% of the given opportunities. Tommy will reduce head
banging, crying/tantrums, and self-stimulatory behaviors 80% from
baseline.

Objectives:
1. Tommy will respond with eye contact when his name is called or when
   "look" or "look at me" is said to him when he is engaged in an activity.
   (achieved and maintaining skill).

2. Tommy will sit at the table engaged in an activity for up to 5 minutes.
   (achieved and maintaining up to 12 minutes with a preferred activity).

3. Tommy will follow 6 one-step instructions. (achieved; has achieved 9 one
   step instructions: sit down, come here, give it to me, stand up, bring it to
   the table, put it on the shelf, throw it away, pick it up, hands down).

4. Tommy will spontaneously point to a desired item when given a choice.
   (achieved; a partial prompt is sometimes needed to shape a point
   response or Tommy will point with his thumb to pictures in a book).

5. Tommy will verbally approximate 3 sounds/words.
   (not progressing; program was put on hold; introduce at a later date).

6. Tommy will learn to match 3 different objects to an identical object.
   (achieved and has learned 6 objects)

Exhibit 2–12a

Practice and Extending Skills

A home-based session in late June proved useful for practice and exten-
sions of achieved goals. He needed full prompting to put one block in the
bucket in his first session with Marilyn in December. Now, Tom was able to
put the blocks in the correct spot on a 6 sided shape box with 18 different
shapes. It was particularly exciting that Tom was now problem solving- if
a block did not fit at first, he did not get upset but continued to try other
holes until he found the one that fit.

Tommy Jekanowski   Six Month Progress Note
Page 2

7. Tommy will imitate 7 gross and fine motor skills.
   (achieved; has learned 13 motor movements with and without objects).

8. Tommy will receptively identify 3 objects/items. (achieved; can identify
   objects from field of three).

9. Tommy will sit at the table and use his spoon to feed himself. (achieved)

10. Tommy will engage in songs, story books, turn taking, and interactive play
    with an adult for 5 minutes without exhibiting self-stimulatory behavior.
    (achieved)

11. Tommy will request by exchanging a Mayer-Johnson icon for a desired
    item. (achieved and generalized)

12. Tommy will walk up and down stairs with one hand held. (achieved)

13. Tommy will decrease head banging, crying/tantrum and self-stimulatory
    behaviors from baseline levels. (achieved)

Other objectives that were achieved are: undressing; appropriate sitting on
the toilet; drinking from a cup without a lid; matching colors - red, blue,
green, yellow, and orange; signing - cookie, mama, help, and eat; receptive
identification of body parts - head, arm, legs, eyes, and toes.

New objectives that have been introduced since April are: dressing -
underwear/pants; toileting training; drinking with a straw; receptive
identification of colors; signing; matching non-identical items; matching and
receptive identification of shapes; and imitation of the preschool song.

Since May Tommy has been moving through the steps of his programs very
quickly. He is generalizing and maintaining the skills he has learned. There
are times when new materials and programs are presented and Tommy will
attempt to scatter the objects off the table and hit you. However, after he
becomes familiar with the program and knows what you want from him, he
enjoys it and gets very excited when he receives reinforcement for giving the
correct response.

Marilyn Murray   6/23/97
Marilyn S. Murray, M. A.   Date
Behavioral Consultant

Exhibit 2–12b

Tom had grown to love books. Pictured here is Tom reading in one of his favorite spots.

We used many different types of children's books in sessions — alphabet books, books shaped like planes, books that made noises, books that had textures, books that were lyrics to his favorite songs and books that had a lot of repetition and humor.

The May Institute, Inc.
May Center for Child Development
100 Sea View Street
P.O. Box 708
Chatham, MA 02633
(508) 945-1147

Home-Based Consultation

Child: Tommy Jekanowski
Date: June 28, 1997
Session time: 9:30am to 12:30pm

A very productive session. I probed some previously learned skills to see if Tommy has maintained and generalized these programs. He was able to complete the six-sided shape box with 18 different shapes with minimal assistance. Tommy would turn the box to find the right shape and if a shape did not fit he did not get upset. He would either try to find the right place or put that shape down and try another one. Tommy did, however, need encouragement to stay at the table and finish the task.

Tommy matched three dimensional letters when an array of three were presented to him. His matching skills have generalized to different materials. Tommy followed all nine previously learned one step instructions. We are going to begin to introduce two step instructions. Tommy was able to attend to a book being read to him for seven minutes. He participated by turning the pages and pointing to objects when asked with minimal prompting.

Tommy had two toilet accidents about an hour apart. We will introduce a consistent hourly schedule. Tommy will continue to wear underpants. We will also continue to have Tommy practice using the toilet icon and sign. During this session Tommy scattered objects off the table three times. The intervention we are using is to have Tommy pick up the items. With a verbal prompt given, he picked up the items and placed them on the table.

Marilyn S. Murray   *July 7, 1997*
Marilyn S. Murray, M. A.   Date
Consultant

Exhibit 2–13

Exhibit 2-13 shows the late June session notes.

July: Using a Picture Board and More Progress!

Tom's sessions in July went extremely well. He showed progress with spontaneous signs, receptive identification of numbers, letters, colors, shapes, common objects, and toilet training. Marilyn and Kathy, Tom's lead teacher, were now overlapping during sessions, once a week, for training and reliability. Marilyn was very pleased to see that Tom had generalized matching and communication skills. She also noted how happy and engaged Tom was throughout the teaching sessions, despite his continued aggression when he did not want to continue with an activity.

The May Institute, Inc.
May Center for Child Development
100 Sea View Street
P.O. Box 708
Chatham, MA 02633
(508) 945-1147

Home-Based Consultation

Child: Tommy Jekanowski
Date: July 8, 1997
Session time: 1:00 - 4:00pm

This was a terrific session with Tommy. Kathy and I overlapped for training
purposes and also for reliability on programs. We alternated running
programs with Tommy. It was great to see that Tommy has generalized the
matching and communication skills he has learned to variable stimuli (i.e.,
materials, people, situations, etc.).

Tommy was very attentive and happy throughout the session. He started off
doing very well with all the motor imitations, even the new ones he was
trying to imitate. He also has learned to self correct himself. We probed
Tommy's receptive identification of the Mayer-Johnson icons on stationary
boards. He was able to locate drink, cookies, popcorn, pretzels, and play-doh.
A portable stationary communication board will be made for Tommy to use
in the car and outside.

During receptive identification of letters and numbers, Tommy was confused
with the instructions "point to ___ " and "give me ___". When I said
"give me B", he would point to the letter B. We will continue to work with
Tommy on discrimination when these instructions are given during discrete
trial teaching. Tommy has mastered and generalized receptive identification
of circle, square, and triangle.

The only problem behavior exhibited during this session was hitting. This
occurred seventeen times and was directed at either Kathy or myself when
Tommy did not want to continue with the activity.

Marilyn Murray   7/11/97
Marilyn S. Murray, M. A.   Date
Consultant

Exhibit 2–14

After using individual pictures with Tom for weeks, he was now
ready for a portable picture board. Marilyn used a computer program to
create the board and brought it to us the next week. The board was made
up of pictures Tom was familiar with. These pictures included words with
the images to help develop his vocabulary.

Exhibit 2-14 represents the last session notes of our home-based
program.

Transition from Early Intervention to Pre-school

The following is a transcription of my letter introducing Tom to his preschool teachers and therapists.

Tommy Jekanowski

Our son Tommy is a beautiful boy, almost three years old with soft blond hair, beautiful green eyes and an infectious belly laugh. Tommy also has autism, a neurological impairment which has interfered with his abilities to communicate, relate to others and learn skills that other children just seem to pick up. Autism is still very much a mystery to the medical community in terms of organic location, cause and treatment, until recently. New research indicates that the neurological differences resulting from autism are located in the cerebellum and may have  its origins in genetic coding. Children and adults previously thought to be uneducable are now enjoying the benefits of earlier diagnosis and education.

Tommy was diagnosed with autism at 27 months of age. Two months later, an intensive home-based teaching program was under way. Tommy has made tremendous progress.

Seven months ago, Tommy had no communicative skill; he now uses about fifteen signs and a growing number of pictures to indicate his wants and needs. At that time he had no play skills; he now plays with many toys and especially enjoys looking at books, using number and phonics machines and puzzles.

Tommy was only bonded to his mother seven months ago–he now very much enjoys his father, brother and several teachers and visiting family members.

Tommy still struggles with learning new skills, imitation is something he still learns for the most part by rote.

Tommy still "stims" on his favorite strap and "postures" more frequently when tired, stressed, or sick.

Verbal language has not progressed since we have

begun intervention but we are encourage by his increasing understanding of language and interest in letters, numbers, and colors. Tommy has enjoyed many talented and intuitive teachers over the last 7 months whose belief in his potential has inspired us all. We are hopeful that his progress will continue this fall when he makes his transition to Kim Albertson's Pathways' team.

TOM'S THOUGHTS

It's astounding to look at the professional notes of all my sessions and how I developed to a more compliant learner. I regret hitting Marilyn and Kathy as I am immensely grateful to both of them for helping me learn. They basically helped me become the learner I am today. I honestly wish I could remember what went down in those sessions, but I was too young to. There are a few characteristics mentioned in this chapter that won't go away. For instance, I still stim to this day as a way to release energy and express myself, but I've been making sure that it doesn't disturb anyone. I also enjoy looking at picture books and chapter books.

REFLECTIVE GUIDE

*Early Intervention for young children with autism (like Tom) teaches foundational skills.

*Educating and caring for a child with autism is an awesome responsibility

*Home programs with consultants may be funded through external agencies

*Be willing to blaze new trails. Advocate for what you believe your child/ student needs.

1. Why is Early Intervention so important for young children with autism?

2. How do we commit and help others to commit to working together to educate a child with autism? What is at stake?

3. What private schools in your area are successfully educating young children with autism? What can you learn from them?

4. In your role as a parent, educator or therapist, how can you advocate and/or join others in advocating for an educational program each child with autism needs?

CHAPTER THREE

The Chicken Chair

Pre-school

At three years old, Tom transitioned into Pathways, a small integrated pre-school with seven students—three (including Tom) with special needs. The Pathways classroom had a lead teacher Miss Kim and two teaching assistants- Miss Meredith and Miss Karen.

In our first IEP meeting to review data and plan for a smooth transition into Pathways, Miss Kim shared that one of her teaching assistants, Miss Karen, would be taking maternity leave. We immediately thought of our own Miss Kathy, who had become the lead teacher for Tom's home program. What an opportunity this would be for Tom's education and care! Kathy knew exactly what Tom could do, what he knew, how he learned best and what motivated him. Not to mention the fact that Kathy was a certified special education teacher with applied behavioral analysis training. Kathy accepted the teaching assistant position for the fall making Tom's transition into Pathways seamless!

Pathways was the beginning of Tom's learning with and from his peers. While Tom was able to learn many behaviors and skills in 1:1 teaching sessions (eye contact, pointing, attending, sitting, rote play skills, taking one and two step directions, receptive language, etc.), his expressive language and social skills developed primarily through his typically developing peers. The constant chatter and social interactions in the classroom and on the playground provided Kathy and Tom with never-ending teachable moments. What better way for Tom to generalize what he was learning than to practice immediately with his peers at school. As Tom learned from them, they were learning from him. Tom was teaching them to include him in their moment-to-moment activities. Far from being a chore, they quickly discovered how fun Tom could be and how great it was when he learned something they taught him. Tom could be frequently found sitting with classmates in the Chicken Chair. Note that in the photo (top of page) it looks like the girls are taking turns reading to him. Tom is allowing them to sit real close, is completely engaged and well, the girls are too.

Tom's IEPs, progress report, daily communication logs and pictures taken during these two years of pre-school all document significant progress. When he entered pre-school at age three Tom's language, eye contact, play skills and tolerance of anyone other than me was still limited. When he finished pre-school, Tom was able to use pictures to communicate his wants and needs throughout the day; his spoken language increased to eight words and his play with others was developing. His circle of friends now included six classmates and two little girls who read to him daily in the "chicken chair." Through his Pathways teachers and classmates, Tom made significant gains in socialization and proved to us all that he was ready for summer school and kindergarten in the fall.

TOM'S THOUGHTS

Ah, I really wish I could remember my preschool years. Maybe they could have been as memorable as my high school/college years and beyond. Speaking of high school, the chicken chair reminded me of another chicken thing that I'll get to in my high school years...

REFLECTIVE GUIDE

*Children with autism (like Tom) learn language and social skills best from/with other children (with teaching support).

*Inclusive education benefits all children in many ways.

*Successful inclusion (like Pathways) is the result of ongoing planning, support and communication.

*Daily communication logs are an important way to keep care givers, teachers and therapists connected and focused on each day's progress and challenges.

1. What kinds of activities and lessons, in an inclusive classroom, could best support the development of language and social skills for students with autism?

2. How does inclusion benefit students with autism? How does it benefit typically developing children? How did inclusion benefit Tom's classmates?

3. In your role, as caregiver, educator, etc. how can you advocate for and ensure that there is adequate planning, support and communication for successful inclusion?

4. In your role, how can you engage others in using a daily communication log?

CHAPTER FOUR

Practicing and Maintaining

Summer School

Tom attended three years of summer school from 1998 through 2000. Along with the IEP team, we asked ourselves: what would it look like? How many days? How many hours? For the first two summers of 1998 and 1999, Tom attended school in the Pathways classroom, five days a week, five hours a day. His classroom teaching assistant, Miss Kathy for the first two years, then Mr. Jym, worked with Tom 1:1 in the classroom and on the playground. How fortunate for Tom that our lovely Miss Kathy taught the first two summers. She was able to provide seamless continuity from the school year to summer school. She knew exactly what Tom was learning

and his preferred teaching materials. She knew Tom and Tom knew her. Tom also had the same occupational and speech-language therapists he had during the school year. Once or twice a week, for 30-minute sessions, each therapist would work with Tom in pairs or in a small group. These small groups were important in helping Tom maintain communication and social skills.

Kathy, Jym, Tom's therapists and our family used Daily Logs, in different forms, to communicate progress, issues or ask questions. Kathy typed weekly summaries of her sessions recording what skills Tom was maintaining, and what skills or concepts she was introducing. Kathy's detailed notes were supplemented by our daily conversations before and after teaching sessions. Jym's handwritten notes included a daily summary of Tom's work, and were organized by subject area (Language Arts and Math).

The Beach

After summer school, we would often go to the beach. Tom loved splashing in the water and building sandcastles. I remember trying to keep Tom's swimsuit on and how, on many days, we just gave up and let him swim naked. It didn't occur to us, until much later, that Tom may have been seeing the ocean as a big bathtub. Because we worked so hard to teach Tom to undress himself before getting in his nightly bath, he may have thought that going to the beach meant taking off all his clothes, which included his bathing suit. He did eventually keep his swim suit on at the beach, but I honestly cannot remember when.

MAINTAINED

Matching, Numbers, Letters, Days of the Week, Months, Rooms and Objects in the Enviornment (Kitchen, Stove, Refrigerator, Sink, Microwave, Dishwasher, LivingRoom, Couch, Chair, Rug, Carpet, DiningRoom, Table , Chairs, BathRoom, Sink, Toilet, and Toilet Paper)

* Tom signed blue and said lamp. He also signed black and said phone, T.V. and Table.

We spelled the names of animalsand labeled pictures of animals(Elephant, Pig, Up, Down). We also maintained Front and Back, Top and Bottom, Full and Empty, Warm and Cold.

FINE MOTOR

We traced a Horse, Goat, and Zebra. Tom said their names. I spelled their names on paper. Tom made horizontal and vertical stripes on the Zebra. We wrapped Two dollars in nickles. We counted 35 nickles.

PHONICS

I used my phonics cards. Tom said hat, cat (ka), toes(we counted toes), and fish. He also thumb, hand, and celery(cel).
While reading a story, I pointed to a word that Tom knew. He would say it . I would repeat it and Tom would say it again. He read cow, pig, horse, skunk, turtle, spider, dog, and bird.

Introduced Opposites and Labeled:

wet/dry, up/down, open/close, stop/go, sit/stand, awake/sleep, full/empty, fast/slow, on/in, off/on, many/few, and under/over.

EASEL

Wrote numbers, drew a horse(prompt), cow, and dog. Tom drew a face. I prompted legs , hands, arms, and feet.

Tom matched an arrangement of 30 cards from a memory game. He pointed correctly to 30 of the total 33 cards.

We played Animal Dominoes, and the Bug Puzzle.

Exhibit 4-1

Exhibit 4-1 is a sample of Kathy's typed notes, followed by a sample of Jym's handwritten notes as Exhibit 4-2. On Jym's notes, I have responded to his question and thanked him for responding to Tom's non-compliance in a game with a meaningful consequence—he would not get to play. We were all on the same page with this response and eventually Tom learned to take turns and enjoy playing games even if he didn't get his preferred color, go first or win.

Monday, July 31, 2000

wed morning Please continue to expect a picture — maybe you could give him a prompt or begin the drawing for him?

Journal — Wrote about watching the Littlest Angel
  — Some non-compliance with the picture. maybe 2 sentences — no picture?
  — Let me know what you think —

Math — identified coins — good job — sometimes confuses nickles and quarters by sight. Started counting dimes by 10 - 10-20-30-40-50 almost got it — gets stuck on 30 — then he can finish.

had trouble playing a game with Chris. They both wanted to be red. Soo Tom was red first — then Chris. Took a small fit when it was Chris turn to be red. Tried to get him to be yellow. He would not comply, so he did not get to play. Thank you!! ti

Exhibit 4-2

TOM'S THOUGHTS

Good old summer school! I keep thinking about one time in summer school where a man (probably Mr. Jym) was saying "lower case" and I said "upper case" but I can't remember the context in which this conversation happened. I read Mr. Jym's notes about me having a fit over not being red in a game with another boy. Now, I really wouldn't care what color I am, as long as I enjoy the game and/or want to play it. During summer school, I found a love for Betty Crocker's "Kid's Cook" that I had until I moved to Florida and pretty recently rediscovered and bought it on Amazon.

I am baffled that I let myself swim naked at the beach on Nantucket! Fortunately, I somehow abandoned that habit before I hit puberty. If I still swam naked at beaches during my teenage years, like I did in preschool, awkward wouldn't even begin to describe the experience! I wore a t-shirt and a bathing suit to more recent trips to the beach.

REFLECTIVE GUIDE

*Data collection/analysis to support the need for summer school begins in the fall.

*Continuity in summer school staff, as much as possible, is a great benefit to student learning (Tom had Kathy and the same Speech-Language and Occupational Therapists).

*Variety in daily communication is to be encouraged, as long as the main thing (in our case, Tom's learning and well-being details) remains the main thing.

*Be specific, clear and supportive in your communication with one another.

1. What data does your child/student generate throughout the school year and how can you make sure that it is being collected and monitored to evaluate the need for summer school?

2. In what ways did Tom benefit from having some of the same staff during summer school that he had during the school year? How could you ensure that those teachers and therapists still get their much needed summer break?

3. In your role, how do you envision the outline/content of a daily summer log? What was the main thing for Tom? What is the main thing for your child/student?

4. How do you think the style of my communication with teachers affected Tom's education? How could it affect those that work with your child/student?

CHAPTER FIVE

See What Tom Did Today!

Kindergarten

Tom transitioned into kindergarten, supported by a team of teachers, therapists and a community of his peers. There were 16 students total with 3 (including Tom) having special needs. The other two students with special needs were developmentally delayed and hearing impaired. The lead teacher, Mrs. D., had taught kindergarten for many years and was joined by a teaching assistant, Ms. S. Learning in their classroom was active and creative. Whatever support Tom needed to engage was provided — peer modeling, visual prompts, hand over hand, etc. Every day, we were enthusiastically invited to see Tom's work, whether it was his morning signature, a journal entry, art project or a polaroid that captured him playing alongside a classmate. Here is a first week project entitled "All About Me."

Tom participated in weekly "specials" such as gym, art and music classes with Ms. S. and his other classmates. Tom loved going to specials. In gym, Tom learned how to throw and catch. He learned how to play badminton and indoor plastic bowling.

In art class, Tom learned how to paint, mold clay and get messy, cre-ating sculptures with paper ma-che. He learned about great art-ists, their work and their lives. In art class, Tom learned that everyone was an artist! His art teacher told him and all his classmates this every day!

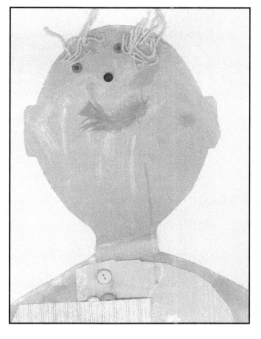

In music class, Tom learned to dance and play many games and songs with his friends. He listened to mu-sical masterworks and enjoyed watching Walt Disney's Fantasia for the first time. He especially enjoyed weekly sing-a-longs with his Dad and the entire kin-dergarten class.

Tom was able to learn in his inclusive kindergarten class-room and all his special classes (gym, art, and music) because of the leadership of Miss Kit, Tom's Special Education teacher. She is the one who helped all Tom's teachers and thera-pists implement his behavior plans. Exhibit 5-1 is the plan that supported Tom's inclusive kindergarten success.

Miss "Must Do"

Miss Kit's data-driven, analytic skill set, was a great asset to the entire team. Every week, Ms. Kit would work with Tom on non-preferred aca-demic tasks. These tasks became known as "must do's." Tom learned that after he did a "must do" fun always followed. Many years later, when we returned to the school and saw Ms. Kit, Tom reached out for a big hug, and through the giggles, greeted her as "Miss Must Do."

At the end of kindergarten, Miss Kit wrote: "Tom had a very produc-tive and successful school year. Tom actively participates in most class les-sons and projects with assistance and prompting. Modifications are made as needed. Tom is becoming more social with his peers. Tom's aggressive outbursts have decreased dramatically in comparison to last year. Tom has become more responsive to verbal requests to act appropriately and his level of impulsiveness has decreased. Turn taking is another area Tom has made great gains in. Through our implementation of board game play-ing with peers, turn taking when reading, turn taking when writing, Tom

Behavioral Modification Plan For:
Tommy Jekanowski
School Year 1999-2000.

Tommy exhibits some inappropriate behaviors. The best way to decrease the probability of these behaviors occurring is through a consistent approach. In order for any behavioral plan to work effectively all the participating staff must be on the "same page". It is vital to always maintain a firm but neutral voice tone when addressing inappropriate behaviors with Tom. On the other side of the coin it is equally important to use a very up-beat tone when verbally praising Tom for compliance and task completion. Voice tone and affect are important as Tom knows the difference between both tones. Keep proper voice tone in mind when addressing Tommy...up-beat when he is being appropriate, and firm BUT neutral when a target behavior is exhibited.

I, as Tommy's behavioral consultant will closely monitor the effectiveness of this program. Give it time, it takes a patient team of people to implement a consistent program. As with any behavioral support plan once the intervention is introduced to the student the severity initially of the behavior may increase, but be patient the contingency task and other preventive strategies should lessen the occurrence of his aggressions. Attached, please find Tom's behavior support plan. Lastly, I thank you for your patience and persevearance as we all continue to work in Tommy's best interest.

-Kit Fruscione, SPED. Teacher
9/27/99

Exhibit 5-1

has become more willing to share and engage in social interactions with his peers. Academically, Tom is progressing along nicely. Expressing his thoughts in writing is an area he continues to struggle with, but through guidance and prompting from his teachers, his thoughts are expressed and put onto paper. It continues to be a pleasure and joy to work with Tom and his TEAM of teachers, therapists and family. I look forward to seeing his continued progress."

Displayed here is a painting that Tom created in art class that year. Exhibit 5-3 shows two pages from Tom's Kindergarten memory book; he included a drawing of his brother Patrick. And I just love that Tom said the best thing about himself was that he was "very nice"!

LIST OF TOM'S EXHIBITED BEHAVIORS
AND THEIR DEFINITIONS:

A. AGGRESSION: The physical striking of a peer, adult with hand, foot, fist, shove, push, slap, done with intent.

B. NON-COMPLIANCE: The refusal to comply to a teacher's directive to participate in an activity.

C. TRASHING: The clearing of an object or materials from the table OR the intentional throwing of an object.

D. SCREAMING: High pitched vocalizations that disrupt the classroom in a negative form, exhibited as an oppositional protest.

WHAT TO DO IF TOM EXHIBITS ANY OF
THE FOLLOWING BEHAVIORS:

A. AGGRESSION- Firmly state, "No Hitting." Escort Tom to designated desk area. Seat him behind table, if he won't voluntarily sit permit him to stand. Place contingency task cannister in front of him, hand him 1 poker chip at a time. Tell him firmly, "Do your work." Continue handing him chips until all 20 chips are complete. Then do what is called a TEN SECOND HOLD- simply count to ten in your head and if Tom is quiet with no yelling or whining return him to an activity. Should Tom not exhibit quiet during the TEN SECOND HOLD he must repeat the 20 chip process until he can meet the criteria of calm.

B. NON-COMPLIANCE- Tell Tom "It is time to do _____ when we're done we can go back to doing ---------(prior activity)." Encourage Tom to participate if only partially.

C. TRASHING- Firmly state, "No trashing" Implement Contingency task (See above letter A.).

D. SCREAMING- If so interruptive to class remove him until he quiets down Although, should he aggress or trash in process implement Contingency Task (letter A above).

Exhibit 5-2

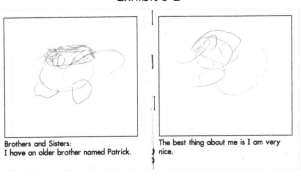

Brothers and Sisters:
I have an older brother named Patrick.

The best thing about me is I am very nice.

Exhibit 5-3

TOM'S THOUGHTS

Kindergarten wasn't a time I remember too clearly, but I can make a few reflections to how it affected me. The fact that going to gym taught me to be more comfortable with higher noise levels benefited me greatly in high school, when I could help create even higher noise levels.

Oh, Miss Kit, aka, "Miss Must Do"... the most memorable part of kindergarten. Miss Kit's term "must do" would be mentioned for the next several years. I saw Ms. Kit the last time in the summer of my high school junior year.

My mom and dad also did sing-alongs with the class. Songs such as "Puff the Magic Dragon", "Daylight Come and me won't go home", and "Bumpin' up and down in my little red wagon" were hits.

REFLECTIVE GUIDE

*Successful inclusive classrooms keep the ratio of students with disabilities, to students without disabilities, low. (Tom's classroom ratio was 3/16 or 19%, which was comparable to his school's overall ratio).

*Enthusiastic teachers who create engaging, hands on lessons are more likely to be successful at meeting the needs of all students. (Tom's teacher couldn't wait to tell and show us what he did every day).

*Supporting students with autism in classes such as gym, art and music is essential to their education. (Tom developed language and social skills in these classes in addition to knowledge of the arts and physical education).

*It is essential for all to effectively address, with the same strategies, the negative behaviors of students with autism. Behavior plans work!

1. What is the ratio of students with disabilities to students without disabilities in your child/student's classroom? If not ideal, how can you effectively advocate for a lower ratio? How early can you begin to have these conversations before the next school year starts?

2. We were not allowed to request teachers by name for the following school year but we could request the kind of teaching Tom needed. How can you work together with educators to articulate what kind of teaching/ teacher your child/student with autism needs in the coming school year? (We met with Tom's IEP team in the spring of every year for this purpose and were happy with the match every year).

3. Art, Music and Physical education benefit all children in many ways. How can you ensure that your child/student with autism has the proper support to be successful? (Tom's classroom teaching assistant provided needed support in these classes and over the years, faded as he progressed).

4. Who is responsible for writing behavior plans for your child/student with autism? How does the IEP team contribute to its draft and implementation? How do you ensure that all educators and therapists are familiar and are implementing said plan?

CHAPTER SIX

Shows Great Enthusiasm!
First & Second Grades

Tom flourished the next two years in a multi-age first/second grade classroom with a lead teacher, Mrs. M. and her teaching assistant, Mrs. L. There were 16 students of which three students (including Tom) were identified with learning disabilities. Tom became increasingly engaged in all subjects and lessons but especially in reading groups. Mrs. M. wrote this on a second grade report card:

"Tom shows great enthusiasm in reading group. He enjoys writing short stories. His oral reading is fluent and comprehension is good. His writing has improved greatly and he is using a wide vocabulary in writing — beginning to use the dictionary. In Math, Tom is mastering concepts easily. He enjoys math lessons and is kind to his peers. Social studies topics covered include: Geography, Native Americans and China. Science topics include: Balance and Motion and Fossils."

Behavior Support Plan
For: Tom J. 11/30/00

Should Tom exhibit the following behaviors please implement the following strategies. Consistency is important in order to help decrease and/or extinguish his inappropriate behaviors.

Non-Compliance- (defined as) student refusing to attempt/complete task, activity, or movement from one environment to the next at teachers request within at least 5-10 seconds of initial command. Should Tom exhibit non-compliance as defined Teacher then should (when he refuses to do class work) say, "Tom either we do it now or we'll do it during recess." Prior to Tom changing environments do provide him with 5 minutes verbal warning that he'll be going to lunch, P.T. etc as so he can then mentally prepare himself. Should Tom refuse to move from one environment to the next go through the hierarchy of prompts, verbal command being the least restrictive, and manual guidance (physically assisting him) the most intrusive. "Tom do I need to help you go to P.T.?" Something else that may work is giving him a choice of bringing a favortie book, toy with him, or being line leader.

Physical Aggression to peers/adults-(defined as) exhibits grabbing, hitting, headbutting to peer/adult. Should Tom exhibit aggression and/or attempt to aggress teacher should intervene remove Tom from close proximity to targetted student and in a frim voice tell him, "No hitting." Tom then needs to apologize to the student. Insure that Tom apologizes while looking in the student's eyes. Praise Tom for times he shares with others and exhibits appropriate touch i.e. (handshakes, high fives, a pat on the back.) Keep in mind Tom's aggressive behavior increases when he is sick. Strategies to implement are maintaining a safe distance (when applicable from peers), when Tom is in the hallway or in line giving him something to carry so his hands are occupied. If Tom's aggression escalates to the point of uncontollable he is to be removed from the classroom to an unoccupied room (sci. lab, Heather F.'s back sppech rm. office until he calms down. Should Tom continue aggressing have Kit Fruscione paged.

Exhibit 6-1

Tom continued to receive weekly behavioral support from Ms. Kit. She was key in addressing Tom's non-compliance and aggression. Exhibit 6-1 shows the plan that was implemented at school. We implemented similar strategies at home.

"Off Island" Evaluations (2000 & 2002)

In the fall of first grade, Tom returned to Boston Children's Hospital for an evaluation to review his progress. While there were significant improvements in many areas, they noted, and we knew, that Tom continued to struggle with less structured and more abstract tasks.

The speech-language pathologist found his single word vocabulary skills were average. It was difficult for Tom to understand directions or commands that were open ended. Also noted were difficulties with sentences, both in understanding and construction. However with structure and repetition Tom was able to follow simple, concrete conversation. Without structure and repetition, he was not...not yet.

Tom's academic skills were varied—reading levels were excellent while math computation was poor. Tom's paper and pencil work were described as disorganized and required much effort. Discrepancies were noted that although word recognition skills were above grade level and decoding skills were at grade level, comprehension was below. On the *Woodcock Reading Mastery Test*, Tom decoded at a second grade level but on the *Burnes Roe Informal Reading Inventory*, Tom failed to pass even the pre-primer passages for reading comprehension. Although Tom's spelling was average, his written expression skills were reported below. Behaviorally, Tom appeared impulsive, requiring repeated redirection to task — often repeating or responding with "yes" after each statement made by the clinician. Rocking in his chair was noted.

Most remarkable from this evaluation in 2000, was the finding that Tom's cognitive functioning, in just three short years (8-month early intervention, 2 years of pre-school and 3 months of kindergarten), was now in the average range. Part of the cognitive assessment evaluated recall or memory. Tom's evaluator concluded that his recall was "low average" and that he recalled information he had heard better than what he had seen. In retrospect, I wish we could have observed this part of the evaluation. I wonder *now* whether other variables were in play. For example, in these tasks testing recall, was Tom able to see the testing script? Tom's sight word recognition was high, so if he had been able to see the script, he could have been reading along with the evaluator. I also wonder what visuals were used to test recall? Were they images or photographs that Tom

Exhibit 6-2

was familiar with or were they ones he had never seen before? To Tom, a picture of a car used in a lesson was a car. In subsequent lessons, we would use other pictures of cars to help him to understand that cars came in different shapes, sizes and colors. To conclude that Tom could recall information better when it was presented verbally, as opposed to using visuals, is interesting. Regardless of my retrospective musing here, this evaluator concluded that this finding was consistent with a diagnosis of autism and we were very pleased that her overall findings confirmed Tom's progress!

Then, at the end of second grade, in the spring of 2002, the IEP team recommended a third, off-island evaluation. We were anxious for an objective assessment of progress to date and our inclusive education model. In the back of my mind, I frequently wondered if we were doing enough. Much to our relief, this report concluded that our inclusive model was proving very effective. Tom had made significant progress managing his autism in these two years since his last evaluation. Tom was described during these testing sessions as very engaged and social. He was also observed flapping and rocking at times which were noted as consistent with his diagnosis of autism.

The speech and language assessment reported wide-ranging levels in Tom's receptive and expressive language skills ranging from above average to significantly below, with impaired pragmatic skills. Auditory memory was within the normal range as were articulation, voice, fluency and rate. Educational assessments included word recognition, oral reading, decoding skills, written skills, written expressive language and spelling skills. They were all noted in the average range. Mathematics were within the average range as well. These results were encouraging and confirmed the data from our school based assessments. Tom had made great gains because of the dedicated and caring team of teachers and therapists supporting him these past two years!

Exhibit 6-2 displays Tom's journal entry during our Spring vacation in Florida.

When Tom was in second grade, I coordinated the religious education program for our local Catholic church. When I realized there were children, including Tom, in our parish family who were not participating in our religious education classes, I designed a multi-age curriculum just for them. With a dear friend Mrs. H., we taught 5 beautiful children ranging in

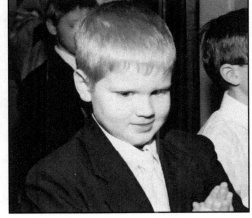

age from 6 to 16 with various disabilities: autism, downs syndrome and mental retardation. Our home, on Sunday mornings, was a one room school house! After class, we took everyone to Mass. In the spring of that year, our 16-year-old friend with down syndrome received the Sacrament of Confirmation and Tom received his first Holy Communion. Tom is pictured dressed in a suit jacket and tie on his special day.

Tom loved art class! Here is Tom's first grade painting. His art teacher, Ms. O. provided the outline. Love, love, love this painting!

During the summer following second grade, friends invited us to a fancy barbecue that, unknown to us, was being covered by the local newspaper. A photographer approached and asked if he could take our picture. I held back from telling him what a miracle it was for us to be out at an event such as this.

The Inquirer and Mirror, Nantucket, Mass.

the Scene

Photo by William Ferrall

Elizabeth Jekanowski with her son Patrick at the Lightship Basket Museum basket-makers' barbecue Thursday night.

Exhibit 6-3

TOM'S THOUGHTS

Mrs. M. and Mrs. L. are the most memorable parts of my first/second grade years. I am so grateful that they were great teachers for me and many other students. That picture I took with my mom and Winnie the Pooh took place after a Norway boat ride with a scary troll. I think I remember being kind of traumatized by that troll, but I'm well over it now. So glad to know that "Frozen" attraction replaced it. P.S. I'm friends with Mrs. L and Mrs. M. on Facebook.

REFLECTIVE GUIDE

*Children with autism (like Tom) show great enthusiasm for learning in classrooms with experienced teachers. Experience makes a difference.

*Behavioral plans, with consistent implementation, support successful inclusion (as it did for Tom).

*Regular and comprehensive evaluations provide objective feedback on your child's/student's progress. (Tom's evaluations confirmed tremendous progress and also areas of continued challenge).

*IEP teams use evaluation data to ensure goals, supports/services and placement for the coming school year are appropriate and effective.

*Religious practice and social outings are important ways for you and your child to be connected to your community.

1. How can you advocate for your child with autism (like Tom) to be placed with an experienced teacher? Why does experience make a difference?

2. Who takes the lead on writing/updating/implementing behavior plans for your child/student with autism? What are the benefits to having such a plan?

3. Comprehensive evaluations can be costly. How can you advocate for these evaluations? Why are they so important and how do they benefit your child/student with autism?

4. Autism can prevent a family from participating in religious practice and enjoying social outings. How can you ensure that you stay connected to your church and participate in community outings? Why is this so important?

CHAPTER SEVEN

Thanks For the Bump, Chuck!

Summer Camp

Tom began attending summer camp after second grade, in 2002. The first year he was an afternoon camper only with summer school in the mornings. The second year, we believed he was ready for all day summer camp. Friends recommended this camp because it of its excellence, its sliding fee schedule and for accommodating children with special needs. The director and lead camp counselor, husband and wife, were special needs teachers who provided their young campers with swim lessons, art class, yoga, field trips and lunch on a different beach every day!

At the time, we were receiving funds from the state for Tom's supplemental programming. The weekly camp fee, on a sliding fee schedule, was covered. Because he would need 1:1 support, we were introduced to

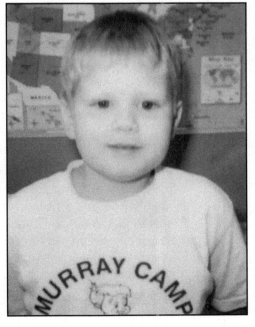

Brittany, a lovely high school student. Brittany was on the island with her family for the summer and was excited to be Tom's camp assistant. She

was a natural! We taught her some simple strategies, sign language and encouraged her to sometimes start but only do for Tom what he could clearly not do for himself. By the second day, they were fast friends.

Every day, we would drop Tom off with his lunch and beach towel and every afternoon we picked him up, Brittany would quickly fill us in on the day's adventures. Brittany made all of the exciting camp activities accessible to Tom. She would hold him up in the pool to practice kicking and arm strokes during swimming lessons. In art class, she would tell us what they learned and what Tom made.

There were board games to play on rainy days, balls to throw at the beach and daily bus rides. While Tom preferred to ride in the front seat with Brittany, other campers quickly discovered the fun of sitting in the back. The dirt roads leading to many of the island's beaches were uneven at best and many had ruts that were quite deep. The best part of the bus rides became driving over the ruts.

The director's husband, Chuck, had a wonderful sense of humor and enjoyed frequent bantering with the campers. So, each time the bus jostled over one of these holes, the campers would shout in unison, "Thanks for the bump, Chuck!" One summer day, while going over a pothole in the family car, we heard Tom shout "Thanks for the bump, Chuck!" Sometimes even today, after all these years, we will be in the car together, go over a bump, and thank Chuck.

TOM'S THOUGHTS

There are a few memories I have of Murray Camp. I remember having a fit when I couldn't be on the same team as Patrick. Now, this is pretty much what I like to call a non-issue. In addition, I also remember a scavenger hunt where I think I found a Rooster of some kind and that the "Rookie" movie was coming out in the movies. Murray Camp was a great way to explore Nantucket Island. It also let me see Joe Zito's cool puppet shows at Children's Beach — fond memories. Oh… and Mac's Place. I wonder what became of Chuck, Brittany and the other counselors at Murray Camp.

REFLECTIVE GUIDE

*Summer camp is a wonderful way to engage children with autism in structured, fun activities with their typically developing peers. (Tom loved it! And continued to make progress over the summer with language and social skills while having fun.)

*Summer camp can be expensive. Seek (as we did) scholarships and funding from local and state agencies/organizations.

*Children with autism may need support to participate in summer camp. Be creative and open to hiring an enthusiastic and responsible young adult (high school /college) to provide this support. (We did and it worked out great!)

1. What are the summer camps in your area that may be appropriate for your child/student with autism to join? What are the benefits of summer camp?

2. Of the summer camps in your area, which ones have sliding fee schedules, scholarships, etc.? What other sources of funding are available?

3. Who can you ask and where can you look for possible young adult support to ensure summer camp success? What do you consider essential qualities of this support person?

CHAPTER EIGHT

True Joy

Third Grade

Tom continued to make progress in all areas in third grade with lead teacher Ms. S.— a new teacher with fresh ideas and enthusiasm for her students—and teaching assistant Ms. L. We were glad that Tom was in such a caring classroom and that Ms. L. was continuing with Tom for a third year. She had bonded with Tom as the teaching assistant in Tom's first and second grade classroom and was incredibly kind and patient. Ms. S. wrote on his report card that he was a true joy to have in class. She went on to write that Tom was such a kind-hearted individual who was admired by all his peers.

Academically, Tom was at or above grade level in all subjects although he sometimes struggled to express his thoughts in writing and his handwriting was laborious.

Exhibit 8-1 shows both his handwriting and his heart.

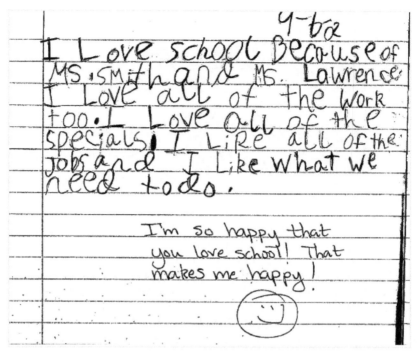

Exhibit 8-1

Tom was also fortunate to continue to have Ms. Kit's behavioral support. Ms. Kit, in consultation with Marilyn since kindergarten, provided clear goals and strategies that helped Tom become increasingly independent and skilled in getting along with his peers. In terms of behavior and social skills, Ms. Kit noted in third grade that Tom was continuing to develop flexibility in social situations—especially when he was not the first chosen in a game, the line leader and/or the winner. Tom was able to walk

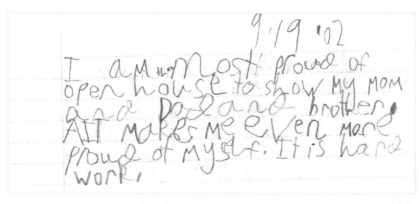

Exhibit 8-2

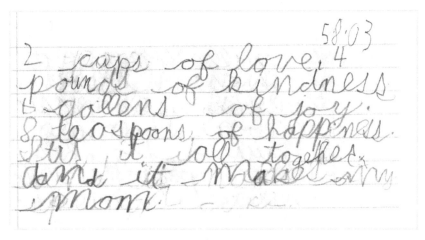

Exhibit 8-3

independently, both with Ms. L. at an increasing distance to class and therapy on his own. Tom was also completing work independently. In her end of year notes, Ms. Kit remarked that Tom's progress since kindergarten had been "a sight to behold." Exhibits 8-2 and 8-3 display pages from Tom's third grade journal entries in which he writes about his love for school, his teachers, and family.

Music

Being Tom's music-teaching-mom for first through third grades was very special. Seeing him walk in line with his friends made me so proud. I can't begin to describe how wonderful it was to teach him and watch him enjoy narrating class musicals, playing instruments, and musical games.

In class, we learned how to read simple musical notation and at the end of his third grade year, Tom presented me with this song displayed in Exhibit 8-4.

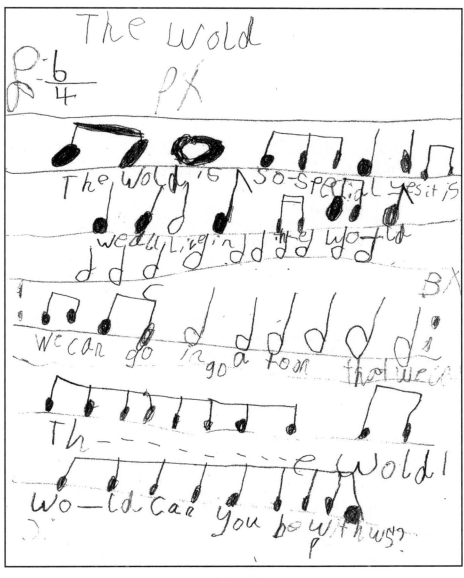

Exhibit 8-4

TOM'S THOUGHTS

I think Ms. S.'s third grade class was the most memorable part of my elementary education on Nantucket. One reason for this was that I still remember the music she played in the classroom. She had Enya's "Orinoco Flow", along with "On Our Way Home," "Across the Universe" and "Blackbird" from the "I am Sam" soundtrack. There were also songs that I remember hearing, but don't know their names.

My mom's music class was another memorable part of my third grade experience. We did multiple plays that year. The picture of me in a red Native American outfit was from a play that told the story of how one Native tribe fought to own the Sun. I think the groups compromised in the end. Another play I remember doing with my mom as music teacher was about a Chinese tale of a boy with a REALLY LONG name. My speaking part involved telling the protagonist "He's standing by the old tree" or something like that. That journal entry I made about loving school was so accurate that it foreshadowed my pursuit of higher education beyond high school. I believe I got the news we were moving to Florida around third grade. Oh the friends I was going to miss in Nantucket. The "For Our Children" album reminds me of my time on Nantucket.

REFLECTIVE GUIDE

*Children with autism love school when their teachers are enthusiastic. Enthusiasm makes a difference. (Tom wrote in his journal that he loved school because of his teachers and still remembers the background music played while they worked).

*Fading support (as Ms. L. did so well for Tom in third grade) to facilitate independence is always the mega goal of all goals for children with autism.

*Music generates powerful lessons and memories for children with autism (like Tom).

1. How can you advocate for your child with autism (like Tom) to be placed with an enthusiastic teacher? Why does enthusiasm make a difference?

2. What are indicators to fade support of your child/student with autism? Why is independence the mega goal of all goals?

3. How can you use music at home and in the classroom to support learning? What songs can be used with the very young to develop communication and language?

CHAPTER NINE

You Should Try Flapping!

Stimming

We had many friends visit our little home on the island over the years. Sue was a visitor and dear friend who loved to knit. One afternoon she was knitting a sweater when 7-year-old Tom wandered over. After studying her for a few minutes, he asked what she was doing. She replied that she was knitting. Then he asked, "Why do you do that?" She smiled and said "I like to do things with my hands."

Tom responded, "You should try flapping." I was amazed in that moment for his curiosity, for the dialogue and for Tom's wonderful self-awareness!

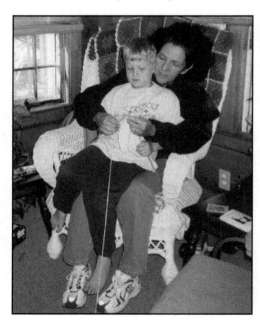

While many believe these self-stimulatory behaviors are for self-calming when stressed or excited, maybe, like Tom, some hum and flap just because they like it!

TOM'S THOUGHTS

Sue is a family friend who visited us on Nantucket
from time to time. I may not have a clear memory
of the previously mentioned moment, but I do remember her visits. However, I still stim to this day as
a way to release energy and express myself, but I've
been making sure that it doesn't disturb anyone.

REFLECTIVE GUIDE

*Individuals with autism frequently stim (repetitive movements, often combined with vocalizations of some kind- humming is very common) when they are anxious or excited as a way to calm.

*Before he was diagnosed, Tom stimmed most of the day. When we started early intervention and our ABA home program, his stimming decreased dramatically. We made it our goal to engage Tom in learning and purposeful play throughout the day, all the while continuing to let him have brief stim breaks. As an adult, he works full time and gives himself short stim breaks as needed. Today, because he cares about how it may affect others, Tom is considerate and thoughtful about the where and when.

1. If your child/student stims, how will you and your team respect and shape this behavior?

2. Why is it important to be explicit and consistent about how you will shape stimming behavior with all teachers and therapists?

CHAPTER TEN

General Education, Please

Fourth and Fifth Grades

At the end of the summer, just prior to Tom's fourth grade year, we sold our home, packed up and headed for Florida. I had been offered a job directing the music program at a Montessori school and Philip was looking forward to part time work.

On Tom's 8th birthday, we enrolled in his new elementary school. This elementary school had an "A" rating for the past ten years! In addition to residency and birth certificate documents, I provided them with a copy of Tom's IEP.

The school secretary was welcoming and assured us that Tom would do well in their autism unit. I quickly explained that, for many years, Tom had been fully included with his peers in general education classrooms and that his IEP was written as such. She let me know that their special education liaison would be reaching out to schedule a meeting to review Tom's IEP and she did. With much conversation and a review of his most recent evaluations, the IEP team concluded that Tom would be in a regular classroom with accommodations and access to special education classrooms for reading, writing and math, as needed.

We met Tom's classroom teacher at open house and were happy to see such a structured classroom! His new teacher was Mrs. A., a nationally board certified teacher who had experience teaching students with autism. We liked her right away! She was clear, direct and consistent. She had high expectations for behavior and learning. Our first impressions proved true as Tom was indeed well educated in Mrs. A.'s class. We were grateful when we heard that Mrs. A. would continue with these students as their fifth grade teacher.

Every year, prior to fourth grade, Tom had a teaching assistant in the classroom to help him as needed. In 3rd grade, need for this support faded to the point of no longer being needed. In Mrs. A.'s 4th grade classroom, there was no longer an assistant- there was one teacher and 20 students. When Tom's first reading test scores came home – 60%, 50%, 80%, we were actually happy because we knew he was earning these grades independently. We realized that in his Island school, all his chapter book reading had been a shared activity and that although comprehension of the story was discussed, he had never taken standardized tests after reading each book. Tom began to bring home chapter books and we began to sit alongside of him, reading our own books silently. Even though his language was still limited, his reading skills were on or above grade level. This practice of reading silently and then taking these standardized comprehension tests was a new challenge! By the end of his fourth grade school year, Tom developed the habit of silent reading during and after school and, over time, began to consistently score 90% and 100% on these comprehension tests.

Written expression was another area that really blossomed for Tom in Mrs. A.'s classroom. While Tom continued to work with occupational therapists to improve his fine motor skills, handwriting was laborious. He was beginning to use the keyboard for some assignments but the majority remained pencil and paper. In the spring of 4th grade, all students across the state took a writing assessment. Tom was given a prompt asking him to write about an important person in his life and explain reasons why this person was important. He wrote two sentences about his new principal saying he liked him very much! On a scale of 1-5, Tom's essay earned a 1. With Mrs. A.'s explicit instruction and practice, by the end of 5th grade, Tom was writing well-formed paragraphs and essays. Tom's next state mandated written assessment in 7th grade showed progress with a passing score of 3.5.

Exhibit 10-1 is a sample of a Thanksgiving essay written in the spring of 5th grade.

Athletics

In addition to Tom's growing academic progress, he was enjoying new friends by participating in Little League Baseball and our church youth

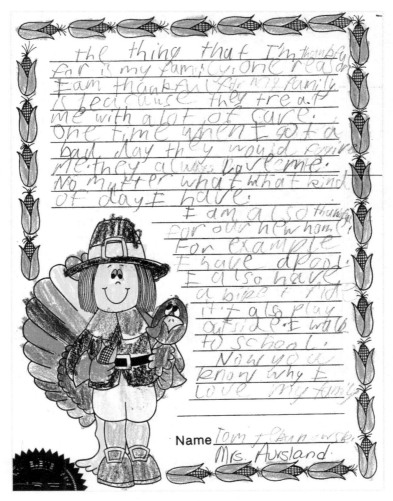

the thing that I'm thankful
for is my family, one reason
I am thankful for my family
is because they treat
me with a lot of care.
one time when I got a
bad day they would comfort
me. they always love me.
No matter what what kind
of day I have.

I am also thankful
for our new home.
For example
I have a pool.
I also have
a bike I ride
it. I also play
outside. I walk
to school.
Now you
know why I
love my family

Name Tom
Mrs. Aursland.

Exhibit 10-1

group. On the Island, Tom had served as a "ball boy" for Patrick's Little League team. In Florida, Tom became a full member of his own team, and would continue for three years.

Tom was excited about going to practice and playing in the games. He developed a special bond with one of his coaches. This coach was also a parent and enjoyed joking with Tom. He knew that Tom was very fond of

rules and doing things correctly. One day he told Tom that baseball was about "lying, cheating and stealing- you know LCS". Tom strongly disagreed and replied "No LCS! No LCS!". To which his coach would say "Oh, yes, Tom, baseball is all about LCS." Tom would start to giggle and repeat "No LCS! No LCS!". They would go back and forth many times the entire season until one of them stopped, usually the coach. Anyone watching and listening to this banter would smile and often cheer for and join Tom in his response.

Tom's teammates were supportive and would always cheer him on when he got up to bat. The first time he hit the ball and got to first base, the crowd erupted as if he had hit a home run! His regular spot was deep in left field. In another game, he caught a pop fly! It ended the inning, the crowd was on their feet! All his teammates signed the ball and it still sits on his desk today. Playing on this Little League baseball team was a wonderful experience because Tom had fun with friends and he was part of a team.

Religious Education

Weekly religious education classes were another opportunity for Tom to be with friends outside of school. When it came to Bible story discussions, Tom was eager to answer questions and enjoyed taking part in the annual Christmas plays. Here is a picture of one performance with his brother Patrick. That year Tom was a shepherd and Patrick a king.

TOM'S THOUGHTS

So, I moved to Florida on the day of my ninth birthday. My mom, brother and I flew to the West Palm Beach airport while my dad drove the moving truck down with a friend. I remember missing all my Nantucket friends, never really suspecting that I would make lifelong friends down in Florida. I remember some of my classmates lived in the same neighborhood I did so we played at each other's houses.

One really fun event I recall is the Mega Bash. It was some kind of fund raiser which offered lavish prizes. However, the music really stuck out to me because it was fun and energetic. Songs like "Macarena", "Cha Cha Slide", and many others played. Another really fun event I remember was a sleep over I went to in Fifth grade. This was because I had a high enough AR (Advanced Reading) score to attend. At this sleepover, I think I saw a talent show or something with songs like "Feel Like a Woman" and Black-Eyed Peas "Let's Get It Started" playing. Another memory from that sleep over was me in a sleeping bag watching "National Treasure" and sleeping on and off through "A Series of Unfortunate Events" movie.

My first time singing in a school choir was in a Christmas/Holiday concert. We sang Christmas, Hanukkah and Kwanzaa songs- I think it was all one song. Little League baseball was the only sport I played while in school (unless you count Marching band, which will come later). My baseball playing years were from fourth grade to sixth grade. I played on the Mets, the Athletics and the Diamond Backs. The coach mom mentioned would frequently tell me (jokingly) that baseball was all about LCS- lie, cheat, steal. If only we knew that pro baseball teams had LCS. One particular example of LCS in MLB in more recent years was an MLB team from Texas, not named the Texas Rangers (hint, they won the 2017 World Series and were accused of sign stealing).

REFLECTIVE GUIDE

*IDEA (2009) prefers regular education placement (with supports and services) for the education of all children with disabilities.

*Many parents, educators, and schools who have not experienced successful inclusion, support separate classrooms as a preferred placement for their child/student with autism.

*Inclusive education benefits all children, and especially children with autism.

1. What experiences have you had with inclusive education? How have these experiences shaped your beliefs about inclusion?

2. If our mega goal is independence and community for our child/student with autism, how does well-planned, well-supported inclusive education help achieve these goals?

3. How can you use your child/student's evaluation and school data to advocate for continuing general education placement? What is at stake?

4. What extra-curricular activities in elementary school would your child/student with autism enjoy? How can you encourage their participation and provide some (just enough) support to ensure success?

CHAPTER ELEVEN

He's the Kindest Kid in School
Middle School

Tom made great gains over his three years in middle school! His transition to his new school went very smoothly. Our elder son Patrick attended the same school so we already knew many of the teachers and were familiar with the campus layout. It also helped that most of Tom's friends from elementary school would be there too.

Academics
Tom continued in middle school with a consultative IEP with some testing accommodations. He did so well in sixth grade that his teachers recommended advanced coursework for seventh grade. Without any supports or accommodations, Tom earned straight A's in seventh and eighth grade advanced classes. The special education coordinator called a meeting to dismiss his IEP. We asked Tom. He agreed. Tom was dismissed from special education at the end of eighth grade!

In middle school, Tom earned Principal's Honor Roll for straight A's and was frequently honored by his teachers as Student of the Month, as shown on the following page. Displayed also is a panel extracted from one of Tom's middle school art pieces—very cool!!!

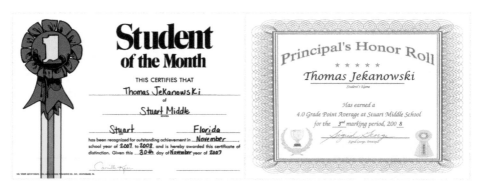

Exhibits 11-1a and 11-1b show a two-page essay that Tom wrote in 7th grade honors English class. Such great progress with his writing! This special notebook paper really helped improve his legibility.

Tom was a volunteer at Camp Invention—a science camp every summer in middle school. He loved it! He is pictured here carrying a bag with the camp director's little dog.

Dad, It's Middle School...It's Never Pretty...

Tom rode the school bus every day. One afternoon, we were waiting over an hour at the bus stop. Because the bus was so late, we called the school office and were told that the bus was delayed because the bus driver had to address some student behavior. When the bus finally pulled up and Tom got into the car, my husband asked him what happened? Are you okay? To which Tom replied "Dad... it's middle school... it's never pretty." And that was that.

Moving Up

Although middle school for most is "never pretty," Tom's three years were incredible and went by very quickly. His 8th grade "moving up ceremony" was held in a packed gymnasium. Phil and I were very emotional as the processional began— another milestone for Tom! As we watched the students processing in, I wondered whether we would see him at all since there were so many people! Then he walked to his seat which was right in front of us!

The ceremony began as they often do with pledges, speeches, and the usual awards. Then each student's name was called as they walked across the stage to shake hands and take their certificate. As Tom's name was called, there was an ovation of applause and cheers! We overheard a mom and her son talking in front of us. She asked him why everyone was cheering for that boy. Her son responded, quite matter of factly, "Oh, that's Tom. He's the kindest kid in the school." Pass the tissues please!

I'll never forget my first year at playing clarinet. My clarinet playing started in 2003, when I was in 6th grade. I was 11 sms at the time. I felt excited about it. I was okay at it, and I got better and better.

My parents bought me my clarinet. My clarinet is kind of old. I was really glad about getting it. My clarinet was also fixed up a little. My clarinet was part plastic and part wood. My parents brought it from Band Box.

I'm a good clarinet player now. One thing that's exciting is that I'm in the marching band. I'm either the first or second (rarely third) person in my block band row. I'm out okay in marching band. I sometimes get out of step, but then

Exhibit 11-1a

I do my best to get back in step. I'm rather excited to be marching and playing. My bandmates and I have to memorize the music.

Also, I occasionally play at church with my dad. My first time playing was at Christmas Eve (on the vigil mass). You may never know when I'm going to play in church next. I was kind of excited about it. My heart was beating when I first played clarinet in church.

I'm so good that I'm first chair in concert band. The reason is because I do my pass-offs (band tapes). I made two mistakes in units four (I had to do units 5-10). I fix those mistakes. Right now, I'm on the last étude (long exercise) of Unit 10. Anyways I'm first chair. That's my clarinet story so far. The End.

Exhibit 11-1b

TOM'S THOUGHTS

My middle school years had some fond memories, classes and friends. I found out that I needed glasses during 6th grade and I've worn them ever since. It's been natural for me to wear glasses except in the shower or when I sleep.

One of the best memories of 6th grade was going to Lion Country Safari. I saw a lot of cool animals and got some nice souvenirs. 7th grade also had its share of nice memories. For example, the picture of me with "What will you invent next?" shirt on was from my time at Camp Invention. I remember the motto "Hey, ho, camp invention got go…." or something like that. I also met two younger siblings of one of my friends who camped there and we bonded.

Some history classes I took in middle school stuck out to me. My seventh grade history class was when I feel like I was introduced to the wide world of history. I first learned about the causes of World War I, World War II, The Russian Revolution and many other subjects. Another history class that was important was my eighth grade American history class. I learned about some Native American cultures along with early American history. In this class, I had classmates who became my friends through high school and even to this day.

My eighth grade science teacher also took out his guitar and played "American Pie" one day. My eighth grade also had a dance class night. This was where I first heard Darude's "Sandstorm," Soulja Boys' "Crank Dat," Fergie's "Clumor," Flo Rida's "Low" and many others.

Band was by far the biggest part of my life in middle school. My band teacher was a great teacher and great human being. Thinking back on it, I think it was really cool that I played band across the street from where I was born. There were also some songs I remembered playing in band: the "Ghostbusters" theme, "Pied Piper," "Dance of the Thunderbirds," "Fair Winds" (conducted by my future high school band director), A Dinosaur Suite of some kind, "Punch and Judy," a spy theme song of some kind, "Under the Boardwalk," and an Avalon song of some kind.

REFLECTIVE GUIDE

*Advanced coursework in middle school may be recommended to challenge (and so engage) your child/student with autism.

*Academic passions (like history and mythology with Tom) ignite and further ignite during middle school.

*Cultivating friendships, through structured, extracurricular activities, is very important for children with autism.

1. Have you or your team considered any advanced coursework to challenge your child/student with autism? Why or why not?

2. What is your child/student with autism passionate about? How can you help further develop this passion through coursework and/or enrichment activities?

3. What structured, extra-curricular activities during school and over the summer in middle school are available for your child/student to nurture friendships? What kind of support might they need to be successful?

CHAPTER TWELVE

Felt it! Kept it! Brought it!

High School

High school was extraordinary for Tom. As a freshman, he joined the Jubilate choir and the marching band. These groups (their directors and fellow musicians) quickly became Tom's extended family. With their support, he grew in confidence and leadership, and developed a vision for college. Tom photos above are (from left to right) Tom as a freshman Jubilate Choir Tenor, a junior-high school band member, and a senior- graduating with highest honors.

In his freshman year, Tom's principal Ms. F is remembered for teaching his science class and providing repeated assurances. Here what Ms. F. shared with me:

> His (Tom's) biology teacher quit the first week of school. So I became their science teacher...and one of these days, I had planned an activity where we were inte-

grated the internet after we completed an assessment. And all the kids were so excited that we were going to go down to the lab and work on this project...that they would be working in pairs, and Tom came up to me... he goes, "what if I don't finish? I need to go to the lab?" and I said, "Tom, don't worry, we'll make time, no matter what it takes, no matter what, we'll get this taken care of"', so he went and sat down and everybody's doing their assessment and, it wasn't a minute later, he is back up at my desk, "Mrs. F, I am really worried that I may not finish this test" and I go, "Tom, its OK, honey. I promise that I will give you the time you need. It doesn't matter, we will take care of it. Whatever you need, even if it is tomorrow, we will work it out. Don't worry, go ahead and get started." And it isn't thirty seconds later, he is back up at my desk. "Tom, what's up dear?" "Well, I really need to be able to get to the lab with everybody." "Honey, I promise, we are not going to leave you behind. You are going to come with us. You get what you can get done now. You are going to be a successful student on this assessment." "Oh, okay, you think so?" "I am certain." "Ok, good." So he went back and sat down and started to work on it.

Here is Tom's freshman assignment in Critical Thinking. I love the way Tom uses these images and colors to express who he is at age 15!

His high school science teacher shared with me how much she enjoyed Tom in her class: one of my favorite experiences teaching Tom was that he would read the information assigned prior to the lecture and would actually research 'fun facts' about the topic.

There was one instance when he brought in his deep sea creature cards to share. We encouraged his sharing because his knowledge was so diverse, and the kids really loved what he had to share.

Tom loved marching band and Jubilate choir! He never missed an after school band rehearsal and quickly became the sweetheart of the Jubilate family. Every time he wore his band uniform and played his clarinet in the stands, on the field, in competitions and in concerts, my heart leapt. During one performance the football field was a mess of mud, but a focused Tom joined his band on the field for their half time show. The music was amazing, but for us, to see Tom move, in step, through this intricate choreography was beyond words! He knew every note and every step! What we didn't realize until later was that Tom's shoe had actually gotten stuck in the mud early in the show. He never looked down or stopped when it happened. Only when he returned to the same spot, in step with the band's choreography, did he put his foot back into his shoe and finish the show.

By senior year, Tom's band director described a leader, well-liked and respected by his peers: *Feel it. Keep it. Bring it.* Those were the words that echoed from Tom's mouth in a way that made every student in the band program smile. Tom would often speak in our coffee-talk sessions that lead up to important performances and competitions with the marching band. He would offer advice or guidance to the younger members who had not been to the event before, but it was the way that he would end his speech with 'Feel it. Keep it. Bring it' that made the speech so much more special. In one instance, the general morale was at a low point. Everyone was exhausted from working so long and so hard on our eight-minute marching show. Tempers were flaring amongst the members and everyone seemed on the edge of collapse. At that coffee-talk session, Tom calmly stood up and told a story about his time with the band. He talked about his favorite moments and how proud he felt to be a member of the group. He ended the speech with 'Feel it. Keep it…. And the entire group of students passionately yelled back, 'BRING IT'. It was a wonderful moment to be a part of and one that instantly boosted the group's morale and sense of confidence.

Here is a transcription of Tom's high school essays on leadership.

Tom Jekanowski
Mr. D.
4/3/11 -
Block 4

If I had to choose the most important part of being a 'good leader,' then it would be impossible because in my opinion there are many important parts. For instance, a good leader needs to have a can-do attitude and be willing to do whatever is best for the whole, not for one's own benefit. In addition, a good leader is expected to work above and beyond "the call of duty" and not abuse authority (i.e. picking favorites and using leadership as an excuse to harass people). Anyone who wishes to practice being a good leader needs to take charge whenever the teacher or director is absent and be honest.

I have had the opportunity to take charge while the director was absent from a band or chorus class. The first time I have done this was when I was in eighth grade when Mr. Hager was absent and the substitute asked someone to conduct. I tried conducting one piece of music, and I think I did pretty well. Another opportunity I have had at leading the band through a piece or two of music or two was last year, my sophomore year, and some of the students told me that I did a very good job at conducting. I have also had the opportunity to lead and conduct my chorus class through warm-ups in both my freshman and sophomore years of high school. Students in that class have told me that I have conducted well. I am also involved in Discipleship Team at Saint Martin De Porres Church, and I have had fun being involved in this group. In all of these experiences, I learned how much I enjoyed being oin a leadership role.

In order to remain in those leadership positions, I needed (and still have) to embody several vital leadership qualities, most of which are values of the band. For example, I am very responsible and honest. I also take my job seriously, but not myself, as well as being willing to work hard in order to get any job done. Band is very important to me for a variety of reasons. Among them are because I have been in Band for so long (the only extracurricular activity since freshman year, and I have been in a band program since I was in sixth grade) and it is a family tradi-

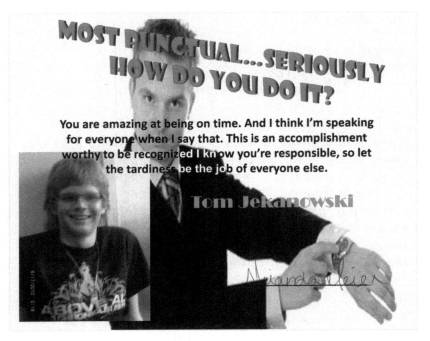

MOST PUNCTUAL...SERIOUSLY HOW DO YOU DO IT?

You are amazing at being on time. And I think I'm speaking for everyone when I say that. This is an accomplishment worthy to be recognized I know you're responsible, so let the tardiness be the job of everyone else.

Tom Jekanowski

Exhibit 12-1

tion to me because my older brother, Patrick, was involved in the Band program.

Leadership itself is a journey in lieu of a destination because leadership is not a, "one-time job," but rather an ongoing position that lasts as long as the program I am involved in lasts.

On a lighter note...this freshman choir award pictured in Exhibit 12-1 speaks for itself.

Tom is pictured here dressed and ready for a marching band performance, and a beautiful letter from his band Secret Santa is displayed in Exhibit 12-2.

Tom loved the business of his high school years. He earned A's in advanced coursework while managing after school rehearsals and weekend performances for band and chorus. As his confidence grew, he started to talk about college.

When we sat with his guidance counselor to plan his senior year schedule, Tom asked if he could take three advanced

Dear Tom,

I couldn't have been more excited when I drew your name for Secret Santa, because I couldn't wait to repay you, in small part, for the entire past three years that I have been here.

There have been multiple times throughout the years that you have inspired and encouraged me, and you probably didn't even realize it. Your positive attitude is so contagious, and your dedication has always encouraged me. You've always only wanted the best for the program, and for other people. I always loved it when you would ask me about leadership and about our marching show and our competitions as we walked out to the field for rehearsal. Because that cheered me up and let me know that someone was out there that enjoyed band and truly wanted us to succeed. And that was exactly what I needed, because it was so easy to focus on all the people who didn't want to be there.

In short, thank you for always giving me exactly what I needed at exactly the right time, even though you probably didn't even know it. Keep doing what you're doing, and keep on being you.

—Your Secret Santa

Exhibit 12-2

placement classes — English, History, and Environmental Science — all in the fall semester. We talked with Tom about the increased homework load of AP courses and his counselor assured us that, if the load was too much, after the first two weeks he could change his schedule back to "regular" coursework. Exhibit 12-3 attests to the excellence with which Tom approached his AP courses. Not only did he handle the increased workload,

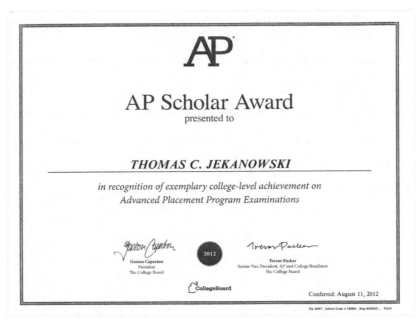

Exhibit 12-3

he earned A's in each course and also passed all three AP exams, earning nine college credits before he even started his first semester in college!

TOM'S THOUGHTS

High school would turn out to be one of the best and most memorable experiences in my life. It helped that many of my middle school friends went to the same high school but I did make lots of new friends. I attended Homecoming dances from sophomore to senior years and prom on my senior year. I remember being asked to do a reading at Bachelorette. As it turns out, my economics/government teacher asked me to read in Bachelorette. The Pastor at my father's church where I went gave the sermon. After graduation, I went to Project Graduation, an all-night party of fun games, food and more. I took some fun pics with friends and tried to roller skate. It's still the latest I ever stayed up.

As in middle school, band was an extremely important part of my life. It all started at freshman marching band camp that took place one week before actual band camp started. I was actually twelve going on thirteen at the time. My 13th birthday took place in the middle of the week so I wore a chicken hat to camp (this now reminds me of the preschool chicken chair previously mentioned). My high school marching band shows were "Illuminations" (like Disney's fireworks show), "Into the Storm", "Harmonic Journey" and "Niagara Falls." I love them all! However, the uniform I am pictured with before my secret Santa letter is actually pretty sweaty when it's hot. After marching band, the musical fun/work was NOT over. I travelled to many places with band such as Disney World (twice), New York City and Atlanta.

My high school competitive choir, Jubilate, was another part of my high school experience. I did not (officially) join until I was in my junior year because I did not get in my sophomore year. Jubilate gave me some great memories to treasure. My brother and I sang in the Men's choir/concert choir when I was a freshman. My senior year involved some epic rapping contest for some of the newer members. The Most Punctual Award pictured here was a time when choir members gave awards to each other. One student gave me an award for being the most punctual. I gave out some of these awards myself. The most memorable one I gave out was the "Swag Award." Like in band, I travelled with Jubilate outside the state to San Diego and New York.

REFLECTIVE GUIDE

*A positive, inclusive school culture is foundational to success for a high school student with autism. (It starts at the top, with the principal. They set the tone and culture for their school).

*High School (and earlier, in many cases) is the time to plan and continue planning for post-secondary goals (college, work, etc.). (Tom decided on college in his sophomore year).

*Advanced placement coursework in high school may be considered for your child/student with autism.

*(Worth repeating) Cultivating friendships, through structured, extracurricular activities during the school year and over the summer, is very important.

1. How does a positive, inclusive school culture support a successful high school education for a student with autism? In your role, what can you do to contribute to a caring high school community of learners?

2. Have you and your team carefully considered every course, every year for your high school child/student with autism? Considered any advanced placement coursework? Why or why not?

3. What structured, extra-curricular activities during school and over the summer in middle school are available for your child/student to nurture friendships? What kind of support might they need to be successful?

CHAPTER THIRTEEN

Independence!
College

Tom set his sights on Florida State University on the way home from dropping off his older brother for orientation. Almost two years later, Tom was thrilled when he received his acceptance letter. He started during the summer semester, which provided him opportunities to become familiar with the campus, classes and college life with a partial credit load and fewer people on campus. We were grateful that Tom's older brother was a student at this University for two years, and so we were ourselves familiar with campus and university systems.

As we helped Tom plan for college life, shopping for XL bedding, new towels and notebooks, we felt strongly about him having a single room. Being on campus, in classes, and often during the day, having his own

room at the end of the day, would allow needed space and time to unwind and decompress. Tom's physician wrote the University a letter stating his diagnosis and verifying his need. Tom was given his own room that summer and every year thereafter.

As a freshman, Tom's major was "undecided." Mid-way through his sophomore year and as he continued taking liberal art courses that interested him, the decision to declare a major in History was obvious. We had

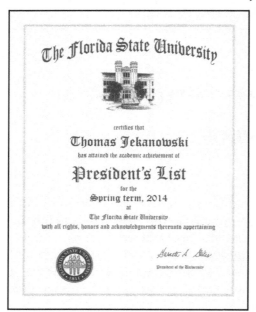

nightly visits on Skype throughout his first year, and weekly thereafter. It was so good to see his face, his smile and to hear updates on cafeteria food, coursework, grades and college events he attended. Tom was diligent in getting his assignmets completed on time and was faithful in attending all classes. We marveled at his ability to navigate large lecture hall classes! While the larger classes would often use quizzes during lectures with "clickers," many of his assignments involved writing papers. Tom was becoming a fine writer—well organized while using and citing supporting resources with increasing confidence. He was also earning high marks, made the President's List, and nominated to The National Society of Collegiate Scholars.

Tom loved college life! Every weekend, there were festivals and events on campus that he enjoyed attending. On our Skype calls, he would show us free t-shirts and swag he had "won." Tom walked everywhere, and this gave him freedom to go to these events as he pleased. He stayed as long or as little as he wanted.

My husband and I would alternate taking the 12-hour round trip for fall and spring

weekend visits. I remember my first trip to meet Tom for Sunday brunch and smiling as so many students, staff and faculty greeted him by name. On another trip, my husband told me about going into the campus post office. While Tom was waiting for a package, a staff member approached to tell him that Tom was the most polite young man on campus. We were so proud of Tom!

While in college, Tom attended weekly Mass with his brother Patrick. He would help with the offertory and, on occasion, join Patrick and his Catholic Student Union friends for dinner. During holiday visits, Tom would join our family's band by playing his clarinet at Mass.

In March of 2013 during the spring break of his sophomore year, Tom joined my husband and me for an Autism conference in Atlanta. I had been invited to lead a session explaining the co-teaching model and its many benefits for students with disabilities. The session began with an overview of Tom's story and concluded with a Q & A session.

Surprised by the turnout, about 75 parents and professionals, Tom and his Dad entered the room just as the Q & A began. I remember that Tom was wearing a T-shirt and jeans, looking just like every other college student! The first question was directed to him. A parent in the audience asked what was his favorite part of being at a University. He paused and looked at me. I smiled and said "They are not asking me. They are asking you." He sighed and, smiling, said "independence." The group erupted into applause, cheers and many stood up to show their enthusiasm. It was quite a moment! They were clapping for him! Standing before them was hope! Meeting Tom in person, as a college student, after seeing pictures and hearing about his diagnosis, prognosis and struggles to learn, was a

thrill and encouragement to all the educators, professionals and families there. After we answered some more questions, and actually ran out of time, lines formed with many who wanted to personally thank Tom and me for our sharing at this conference.

Tom has a cousin who is a singer, songwriter and performer. Growing up together on Nantucket, they were in the same grade but never in the same classroom. Our families shared birthdays and holidays together. In the fall of Tom's sophomore year of college, she invited us to a performance in Orlando. We were so excited, arriving 3 hours before the show, hoping to visit. Her agent texted us to meet them in the hotel lobby. Patrick and Tom were walking around together when the elevator opened. She screamed "Patrick and Tommy!!!!!!!!!!!!!" After much hugging, her agent reminded all of us she was on a schedule and it was time to go.

Tom was so happy to see her and be a part of the evening! When we arrived at the venue, prior to the concert, she was scheduled for a radio show. Tom watched the interview intently from the next room. After the interview, we took some family pictures. Shown on the previous page is one of my favorite pictures of that evening. Except when she was on stage, Tom stayed by her side the entire night! Usually, Tom was good for about 30 minutes at family gatherings before excusing himself to go for a walk. Tom never took a single break that evening. What a gift!

In the spring of his junior year, Tom received a letter in the mail inviting him to join the Phi Beta Kappa society, the oldest, and many consider the most prestigious honor society in the United States. When we talked with Tom about attending the induction event at the house of the University President, he asked the all-important question: will

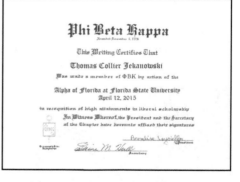

there be food? Yes, we assured him, on the invitation it states that there will be heavy hors d'oeuvres.

In our Skype the next day, he told us he had enjoyed himself very much! He had met and talked with many students and faculty and he had even approached and personally thanked the President of the University for his hospitality! We were so happy that Tom had enjoyed the event and seemed to be so comfortable with other hard working, bright people like himself.

Tom's graduation from Florida State University was surreal for us. Tom, in his cap and gown, honor tassels and big grin was amazing! Here was our son who had graduated with the United States' oldest and most prestigious academic honors, Phi Beta Kappa and Summa Cum Laude, from a prestigious university. It was an absolute miracle! In a packed auditorium, with thousands of other students, families and faculty, we were there to celebrate Tom's college graduation milestone. As his name was read and Tom crossed the stage, we cheered and clapped and thanked God for bringing us to this place.

TOM'S THOUGHTS

At first, I didn't know where I wanted to go to college. I just wanted my own college experience but to stay in State. St. Leo's near St. Petersburg looked like a possibility before I chose The Florida State University. I started in the summer (where I was 17 in college, wow!) which gave me time to navigate the campus. There were also several of my high school peers who went to FSU as well. I also made plenty of new friends in college, including my suitemates/classmates. One of my favorite things about college life was having freedom to meet new/old friends at restaurants and the Suwannee Fresh Foods dining halls.

There were quite a few fun classes I took. Some of them included World Mythology, Classical Mythology, Dinosaurs/Disasters, Religion/Fantasy, Ancient World in Film and an epic sci-fi literature class. I made friends in my classes via study groups and was even comfortable getting in cars with some of my classmates if we needed to go off campus.

One summer in college years, I volunteered at an elementary reading camp for two weeks. This was because there were 3 students with autism... like me. However, I helped the children with their reading. When I think about the younger children with autism at that camp, I wonder to myself, "so this is what it must've been like dealing with me when I was young."

I am so amazed/proud to have a cousin who's a big pop star. You go girl!

REFLECTIVE GUIDE

*Summer semesters are a great way for incoming freshman with autism to ease into college life with a lighter course load and fewer people on campus.

*Single dorm rooms on campus allow privacy and space for students with autism to decompress.

*Walking campus together, before classes start, to practice daily routes to and from classes, cafeteria, library, and campus store promote the student's confidence.

1. Congratulations on your acceptance! Before sending the deposit, is summer semester an option at this university/college for my child/student with autism? What is the minimum summer course load? How many days before semester begins can my child/student move in? what cafeterias/restaurants (days/times) are available prior to the start of classes?

2. Before sending the deposit, are single dorm rooms available? What documentation is needed to qualify for a single room?

3. What are the hotels near campus (walking distance preferable)? Can you or your spouse take a few days off to practice walking routes before classes begin?

CHAPTER FOURTEEN

Can I Help You With That?

Graduate School

Tom moved home after graduation and before he could unpack the first box, we started talking about what was next. He was very interested in graduate school. With three of us in graduate school in the fall (Tom, Patrick and me), the idea of Tom living at home and commuting to a closer university seemed a strong option. Tom agreed and in the fall started a master's degree program in history at Florida Atlantic University. My husband and I took turns driving the 1-½ hour commute each way for Tom's evening classes that first fall. Even though we had a lot of fun on our car rides, we were grateful when he made plans to secure his own room for the spring semester.

For the next year and a half, Tom enjoyed living in an apartment on campus with his own room. I would often meet Tom for lunch or dinner, as his schedule permitted and these were wonderful visits. We would talk about his coursework, campus events, and how he enjoyed serving as a lector at campus Mass.

Graduate coursework in U.S. History consisted mostly of reading, researching and writing papers. One weekend Tom was home, he noticed me writing a proposal for an upcoming conference. I had been writing this particular paper all week and was just getting up, exhausted and spent. With seventy words over the limit and a looming deadline, I was feeling immense pressure. Tom asked if there was anything he could do to help. I thanked him politely but said no. When I explained what needed to be done to meet the deadline, he offered to help reduce the word count. When he offered that, I said "yes, please."

Tom reached for my laptop and began working. Getting up to go to the kitchen, I asked him to please save my copy and create a new copy with his edits. He nodded yes, without lifting his eyes from the computer. I was grateful for the help. About 5 minutes later, Tom called me back to see what he had done. Was this what I had in mind? I looked over his work and was stunned! In this short time, he had already saved my draft 40 words. He had deleted repeated words and phrases, changed passive to active voice and corrected punctuation in several spots. Where had he learned this? He explained, quite simply, that he did this all the time in his graduate courses. I smiled, asked him to continue editing and to let me know when he finished.

When Tom called me back about 45 minutes later, he was beaming! I started to laugh and cry at the same time! He had gotten me well under the required word limit, making room for another 80 words that could be used to strengthen my conclusion. I asked Tom if he enjoyed doing this and he told me "yes, very much." Immediately, I thought of my dissertation editor and wondered if Tom would be interested in learning more about professional editing. His "yes" and wide smile and celebratory pacing was more than enough for me to email my editor and friend Rivka. Her response was a resounding "yes".

Rivka met several times with Tom over his second year in graduate school to teach the essentials of editing scholarly papers using various systems (MLA, APA, etc.). She also showed him how to set up his own editing business (website, fees, payment system, etc.). On Nov 18, 2017, at 12:07 PM, Rivka wrote: FYI, I know I don't need to do this, but I wanted to at least show you my communication style with Tom. BTW, he sounds absolutely lovely on the phone! Here's what she wrote:

November 20, 2017
Hi Elizabeth,

Tom was great, I did not need to take my time really, he got it, and fast. Maybe too fast, lol! He said he had no questions...but I will email him shortly to let him know he can ask me anything at any time.

90 minutes is too long though, there was quite a bit of yawning and staring beyond me after about 50 minutes, he tried so hard and was so polite, but I'm sure it was a hard for him to stay focused at that point. So let's cut it to 1 hour per session, ok?

He was most engaged when he could play with the tools a little bit. I think our best used time together will be in the practice editing sessions.

He needs an updated version of Microsoft Word now, which I believe he has. He will need to purchase Adobe Acrobat Pro (you can find a student digital download for about $XX once he gets started).

His investment in starting his own freelance editing business, which he really seemed to get excited about, will be about $XXX-XXX (Adobe, bizcards, Turabian manual). Not too bad, he can make that money back with his first editing job.

I did give him a homework assignment:

1. to create his own free website for me to review with him (using Wix or Wordpress) at our next session.

2. to design a business card that matches his website (not to exceed $XX, and I led him in the direction of a good company to use - Vistaprint).

3. to purchase Kate Turabian's book that the Dept. of History uses for thesis formatting. Dr. K. thought he might already have a copy, but Tom was not familiar with it. It's about $XX on Amazon.

We left the next session open. I'd like him to finish off his semester strong, maybe work on the homework after finals. But I'll let him decide when we do session 2. A working draft of our schedule is in his binder I made for him. When he's ready, the next session will cover a review of his selected branding materials, a breakdown of editing jobs, and creating a work plan.

Let me know if you have any questions or concerns.

Best,
Rivka

And again:

January 22, 2018
Hi Elizabeth,

It's a true pleasure working with Tom! I look forward to seeing him again!

Best,
Rivka

Spring 2018 was an action-packed semester for Tom. In addition to completing his sessions with Rivka, he joined me as a featured speaker at the Center for Autism and Related Disabilities (CARD) Annual Leadership

Breakfast. Always enjoying the opportunity to present at conferences, I especially cherished this one with Tom. He preferred me going first, so I did. I spoke briefly so that Tom could do most of the talking. He spoke about his life with autism, how much he enjoyed being independent and living on campus as a graduate student. When he finished speaking, he walked over to hug me. There was a standing ovation!

Also that semester, Tom and I served as panelists at a College/Graduate School CARD conference event. Speaking on the phone the night before, Tom asked me what he should wear. I told him he could wear whatever he liked and that I would be wearing a dress and blazer. Picking him up the next morning from his dorm room, I smiled. Tom was wearing a royal blue dress shirt and black pants. I was wearing a royal blue and black dress with a black blazer. When we arrived, our friends asked us if we had planned to dress alike. No, but I guess being as close as we are, it just happened!

Exhibit 14-1 shows the CARD flyer about Tom as we advocated for CARD funding at the state capital. CARD was helping Tom start planning for his transition into work and a career. Tom was planning to join us but, at the last minute was unable to. He did join us in spirit however, through his story on this flyer which I shared with many legislators and anyone, in fact, who would listen. It was an honor to spend the day with our CARD friends and families.

Our friends at CARD were so supportive of Tom! After finishing his editing training and graduate degree, CARD director Maryellen offered Tom the job of editing their Handbook Manual. It was now summer and he was thrilled to start work as a professional editor! I was grateful that Tom continued to edit my conference proposals as well.

I always brought his business cards with me to meetings and conferences. At some point in our conversation, I would introduce my son, the editor. If they had a future need, his work was excellent and reasonable. Returning home from a meeting in our state's capital, I received an email from a well published scholar asking if Tom could help her edit an upcoming journal article. Tom emailed her a menu of his editing services and rates. She quickly responded with an attached draft, specifying what level of editing she needed, and a deadline. He did as he said he would, and even delivered the work early. She praised his "great eye"!

In that same summer, Maryellen, suggested Tom look into Vocational Rehabilitation (VR) for job coaching support. This was an excellent lead! VR would support job coaching programs that would meet Tom's needs. During the six-week VR eligibility determination, we discovered job coaching programs offered through ELs for Autism in nearby Jupiter. Their supportive, autism-friendly training programs looked promising and they were accepting applicants for January through May. By early December,

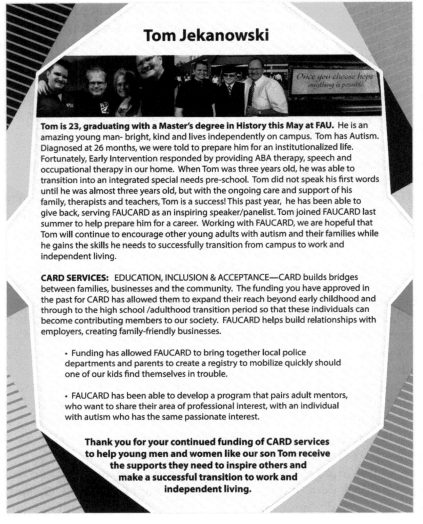

Tom Jekanowski

Tom is 23, graduating with a Master's degree in History this May at FAU. He is an amazing young man- bright, kind and lives independently on campus. Tom has Autism. Diagnosed at 26 months, we were told to prepare him for an institutionalized life. Fortunately, Early Intervention responded by providing ABA therapy, speech and occupational therapy in our home. When Tom was three years old, he was able to transition into an integrated special needs pre-school. Tom did not speak his first words until he was almost three years old, but with the ongoing care and support of his family, therapists and teachers, Tom is a success! This past year, he has been able to give back, serving FAUCARD as an inspiring speaker/panelist. Tom joined FAUCARD last summer to help prepare him for a career. Working with FAUCARD, we are hopeful that Tom will continue to encourage other young adults with autism and their families while he gains the skills he needs to successfully transition from campus to work and independent living.

CARD SERVICES: EDUCATION, INCLUSION & ACCEPTANCE—CARD builds bridges between families, businesses and the community. The funding you have approved in the past for CARD has allowed them to expand their reach beyond early childhood and through to the high school /adulthood transition period so that these individuals can become contributing members to our society. FAUCARD helps build relationships with employers, creating family-friendly businesses.

• Funding has allowed FAUCARD to bring together local police departments and parents to create a registry to mobilize quickly should one of our kids find themselves in trouble.

• FAUCARD has been able to develop a program that pairs adult mentors, who want to share their area of professional interest, with an individual with autism who has the same passionate interest.

Thank you for your continued funding of CARD services to help young men and women like our son Tom receive the supports they need to inspire others and make a successful transition to work and independent living.

Exhibit 14-1

Tom was eligible for VR support and registered for an ELs job coaching program.

In January and February, the first part of his Els job coaching, Tom worked for The Town of Jupiter Building Department, uploading and reviewing information in existing building permits through an online repository. The other two young adults in the program did sorting and filing. Tom loved this program! Every night, he packed his lunch and every day, insisted on looking professional by wearing a dress shirt, dress pants and dress shoes.

In March and April, Tom worked in the stocking and delivery department of the Jupiter Medical Center. With a different coach but the same two friends, Tom learned how to process orders, pack and deliver medical supplies to various locations all over the hospital. One day, I arrived early to pick him up, and his case manager was sitting in the lobby. I thanked her for all the support she and others had given Tom through this job coaching program. She was a huge fan of Tom! Already composing a letter of recommendation for him, she told me of his kindness, consideration and work ethic, not to mention how quick he was to learn whatever systems or protocols were involved in the jobs at each location. With tears of joy, I was overwhelmed with gratitude for the continuing miracle of Tom's life and for the caring professionals continuing to help along his path. She wished us well in our upcoming move and was supremely confident that Tom would find work and be successful wherever he would go!

TOM'S THOUGHTS

I thought that graduate school was the best option for me. It allowed me to further expand my interest in history, plus, it also let me experience some more independence. I lived at home during my first fall semester, but there were days that I went to the Jupiter campus library to relax, walk or work. I had great opportunities to make friends in my graduate courses as most of the classes had most of the same people in them. By the time of my first spring grad semester, I had my own apartment, but I shared a common space with another person. We got along well. As I did with FSU, I fell in love with walking the FAU campus on my own.

Dr. Felsher was a good teacher who taught me about professional editing. She gave me clear guidelines which included cleaning up grammar and making thesis papers sound better. My future editing work for my mom and FAU CARD made me feel as though I contributed a service to society.

REFLECTIVE GUIDE

*Graduate school is an opportunity for adults with autism (like Tom) to further their passion for history and/or other subjects and live independently.

*Utilize contacts and agencies to plan for employment after graduate school.

*Serve as a guest speaker or panelist to inspire younger children with autism and their families.

1. What are nearby universities with graduate programs that could further your young adult with autism's passions? Is it possible to meet with some professors you may be interested in taking classes from, should you go there?

2. Who do you know at this university and other nearby agencies that could help your young adult with autism plan for work support, either on site job coaching or setting up a small business from home?

3. Are there any local or nearby organizations, conferences, etc. where you (you and/or your young adult with autism) can offer yourself as a guest speaker or panelist to share your inspirational story? If you aren't normally comfortable doing this sort of thing, are you willing to do so, with support?

CHAPTER FIFTEEN

We Just Love Tom!

Transition to Work

We arrived in our new home in early June and Tom's job search was on! Every day, he was checking a couple of on-line job portals. Initially, Tom was looking for library and re-search positions at nearby Universities. As he waited to hear back from applications he had submitted, Tom and I scheduled an appointment with Vocational Rehabilitation Services in our new town. Tom's new case manager, Helen, interviewed us both and encouraged Tom to keep applying for jobs to local businesses.

As Tom's job search continued, we talked about expanding to include positions that were similar to his job coaching experiences, e.g. data entry positions and hospital supply stocking/delivery. Mid-July, Tom applied for a local data-entry, customer service job. The next day, he received an email inviting him to an automated interview. Tom asked me to be with him while he made the call. I assured him that he would do great! I encouraged him to listen to the questions carefully, answer them completely and to be himself. Tom took these suggestions to heart and completed the interview very well. Within five minutes, he received a phone call scheduling him for an in-person interview scheduled for the next day. Following the in-person interview, Tom was offered the position. In his acceptance email, he let his new employer know of his VR status. His VR case manager Helen was elated because Tom's hire started a relationship and opened doors of opportunity at this company for others.

Fridays are pizza night. One Friday my husband Philip, waiting in the lobby to drop off pizza for Tom, introduced himself as Tom's dad. The front desk clerk was quick to remark how much they all loved Tom, and what a delight he was to work with. Any parent is happy to hear that but we're especially so. One November evening, while we were away at a conference, Tom let us know that he had won a turkey. What should he do with it? Put it in the refrigerator and help us cook it for Thanksgiving! Tom was very proud! Then, in January, he was awarded "Employee of the Month" with gift cards and use of a parking place right next to the front door! Tom had proven himself a valued employee.

TOM'S THOUGHTS

Getting a job was the most important thing to do after graduating FAU with a Master's degree. I think I had a pretty good resume with the high academic marks I earned in undergrad/grad school. However, I had no experience in a professional environment. This is where Vocational Rehabilitation and ELs for Autism came in. ELs for Autism provided with me with valuable work place experience working at the Jupiter Town Building and Jupiter Medical Center. In the town building, I mainly took staples out of packets, inked seals and went on the computer to process work reports. While at Jupiter Medical Center, I delivered supplies around the office, taking supplies from the warehouse, and crushing bottles in the compactor. The internship would end up being the last thing I did in Florida.

My family and I moved to Iowa on Memorial Day. We initially lived on my mom's college campus until we bought a house in mid-July. During this time, I looked for work until American Customer Care hired me as a Customer Service Representative. Like in school, I asked for help at my new job, as needed, until I got what I was looking for. My co-workers were fun to visit and talk with. There was good music playing where I worked. I enjoyed going to the office, but, everything changed with the COVID pandemic. As a result, I began working from home as of late March 2020. I enjoy working from home and I have been working like this ever since.

REFLECTIVE GUIDE

*Vocational Rehabilitation (VR) is a federal-state program that helps people with physical or mental disabilities get or keep a job.

*Local agencies, such as ELS for Autism (Jupiter, FL) and Goodwill (Iowa), may coordinate with VR to provide job coaching in local businesses to help young adults with autism learn work skills and develop confidence.

*Job sites online, like Indeed, post positions with basic descriptions, salary and benefit information.

1. What is the contact information for your local VR office? How long does the process usually take from application to eligibility determination? What do I need to bring to the first meeting?

2. In addition to VR counselors, who else can you reach out to for nearby job coaching for young adults with autism? For guidance on possible home based business?

3. Is your young adult's resume up to date? Do you have at least 3 references with contact information included on your resume? Is there anyone to practice a mock interview with?

CHAPTER SIXTEEN

Final Thoughts

Tom and his brother, Patrick moved into their own apartment nearby this year. They are great friends who share many hobbies. Tom will always have his family's love and support and will continue to live a life of purpose and goodness.

We hope that anyone who reads Tom's story will be encouraged and inspired. We also implore you to be committed in working together as a family, with professionals and community members, to do whatever it takes to succeed regardless of the challenges or prognosis. Through God's grace, we did. Because of the efforts of so many and especially Tom himself, Tom makes the world better wherever he goes!

TOM'S THOUGHTS

Wow... my life has been an amazing journey! The most recent destination was Iowa. I honestly love living here due to its urban and natural beauty. My brother and I enjoy going to the National River Museum, the nearby Riverwalk, Eagle Point Park and the Mines of Spain National Monument. My life is far from over, in fact, it has just begun, and I'm sure it will have many more challenges as well as opportunities waiting for me.

REFLECTIVE GUIDE

*Dr. Jekanowski welcomes invitations to speak with small and large groups of parents, educators and other professionals about her experiences and expertise with autism, inclusion and other special education topics.

*She can be contacted via email: jekfla3@bellsouth.net.

*To purchase additional copies of this book:
https://www.divinapress.com

1. How has reading Tom's story inspired you?

2. What have you learned?

3. What will you take away, put into practice and share with others?

4. Is there anything you would like to know more about?

ADDENDA

Resources

(in order of appearance)

The Autism Research Institute
   https://www.autism.org/diagnostics-checklist/

Autism Speaks
   https://shop.autismspeaks.org

Cure Autism Now (CAN)
   https://www.guidestar.org/profile/95-4542637

Boston Children's' Hospital
   https://www.childrenshospital.org/#

Franciscan Children's (Boston)
   https://franciscanchildrens.org/

Early Intervention (Hyannis, MA)
   https://disabilityinfo.org/records/cape-cod-islands-early-inter-vention-program/

Applied Behavioral Analysis (ABA for children and adults with autism)
   https://www.autismspeaks.org/applied-behavior-analysis-aba-0

Behavioral Intervention for Young Children with Autism (1996)
   by Catherine Maurice (Editor), Gina Green (Editor), Stephen C.
   Luce (Editor)
   https://www.amazon.com/Behavioral-Intervention-Young-Chil-dren-Autism/dp/0890796831

The May Center in Chatham, MA (School and consulting services for children and adults with autism)
https://www.mayinstitute.org/

The New England Center for Autism
https://www.necc.org/

The Boston Higashi School for Autism
https://www.bostonhigashi.org/

The Murray Camp (Nantucket, MA) (Summer camp on Nantucket Island)
https://www.murraycampnantucket.com/

Nantucket Public Schools (Nantucket, MA) (Elementary School amazing teachers and special education staff!)
https://www.npsk.org/

ELS for Autism (Jupiter, FL)
https://www.elsforautism.org/

Vocational Rehabilitation Services (Stuart, FL)
https://www.servicesource.org/service/vocational-rehabilitation-services/

Martin County School District (Stuart, FL)
https://www.martinschools.org/

Center for Autism and Related Disabilities (CARD, Florida Atlantic University)
https://www.fau.edu/education/centersandprograms/card/

About the Author

Dr. Elizabeth C. Jekanowski is a loving wife, mother, educator, scholar, and presenter with over twenty years of experience in the field of education. Inspired by her son Tom's diagnosis of autism in 1996, Elizabeth embarked on a journey of research, practice and presentations focused on improving inclusive education for students with disabilities.

Recognized as Martin County Teacher of the Year in 2011, Elizabeth has presented at both state and regional conferences, sharing her son Tom's amazing story and the successful evidence-based strategies used by his educational teams.

In 2015, Florida Atlantic University honored her as The Department of Educational Leadership and Research Methodology Graduate Student of the Year and in 2016, Elizabeth was awarded a David L. Clark Scholar distinction for her dissertation "District Leadership and Systemic Inclusion: A Case Study of One Inclusive and Effective School District."

Elizabeth has presented at national conferences. She has been invited to share her research at The University Council of Education Administrators in Denver (2017), and The American Educational Research Association Annual Meetings in NYC (2018) and Toronto (2019). Elizabeth's research was featured at the AERA Special Education/Inclusion Special Interest Group in NYC. She has also presented her research at The Consortium of the Study of Ethics and Leadership Annual Conferences in Education in Houston (2018), Chicago (2019), and Atlantic City (2020).

Elizabeth serves as an expert peer reviewer for AERA, UCEA and The Journal of Research for Educational Leadership for papers on leadership and inclusive education.

Elizabeth has been a board member of The Center for Autism and Related Disabilities at Florida Atlantic University, and along with her son, Tom, been a featured speaker at their annual autism leadership breakfast.

Dr. Jekanowski grew up in Cornwall, Vermont on a small apple farm. Her father, Dr. Theodore A. Collier, was a beloved doctor, in Middlebury, Vermont. Her mother, Joan H. Collier, was a retired nurse who served the local schools and communities. Both parents are deceased. Elizabeth has three sisters: Nancy Rizner of Proctorsville, Vermont, Anne Collier (deceased), and Jane Boucher (deceased). Elizabeth is blessed with eleven nieces and nephews, and five cousins.

Elizabeth attended grammar school in Cornwall, Vermont and middle/high school at Middlebury Union High School in Middlebury, Vermont. Active in school government, she played varsity sports and graduated high school with highest honors. She went on to earn her Bachelor of Arts in American Studies from Colby-Sawyer College in New London, New Hampshire where she received the Carl M. Cochran Department Award. In 2001, Elizabeth completed her Master of Arts in Education from Cambridge College in Boston, Massachusetts and became certified to teach elementary and K-12 music education. In 2003, she earned Special Education certification and in 2015, qualified for Educational Leadership certification. Dr. Jekanowski earned her doctorate degree in Educational Leadership from Florida Atlantic University in 2016 with the Departmental Graduate Student of the Year and the competitive David L. Clarke Scholar awards. Dr. Jekanowski enjoyed teaching at universities in Florida and Iowa, and leading graduate programs as a Coordinator, and then Director of Graduate Programs in Education. She expanded graduate programs at both universities with new partnerships and her students—at both the undergraduate and graduate levels—have praised her support, insight and passion for educating all children.

Dr. Jekanowski began her career as a professional musician with her husband Philip on Nantucket Island, Massachusetts. For twenty years, Elizabeth and Philip entertained at The Harbor House Hotel, volunteered at Our Island Home and various church fairs, while serving as liturgical musicians at St. Mary's Catholic Church. They also entertained in Jupiter and Palm Beach, Florida at Old Marsh Golf Club, the PGA National and many other golf clubs. Elizabeth and Philip served as liturgical musicians at St. Peter's Catholic Church under the direction of Lisa Buckeck.

Elizabeth lives in Stuart, Florida and is married to her soul-mate Philip Jekanowski. Together, they serve as music ministers at St. Lucie Catholic Church in Port St. Lucie, Florida. She has two sons who bring her more joy than she could ever have imagined! Patrick is a Music Director with a Master of Arts in Sacred Music from Catholic University and Tom is a Professional Editor with a Master of History from Florida Atlantic University. Elizabeth is a woman of faith who enjoys helping others, visiting with family and friends, making music, reading, writing, taking long walks and going to the beach.

Dr. Jekanowski consults with individuals, groups, schools, and organizations who serve children and young adults with autism.

CPSIA information can be obtained
at www.ICGtesting.com
Printed in the USA
BVHW052236060522
636033BV00001B/1